Praise for Brain Makeover

"Simple and Powerful!"

> — **John Gray, Ph.D.,** #1 New York Times *bestselling author of* Men Are from Mars, Women Are from Venus

"If you want to learn how to lower your stress, but you're limited on time, look no further. Phyllis Ginsberg provides simple and easy exercises that fit in with your busy lifestyle."

> — **Leslie Reitzes**, Community Manager, Victory Space

"Start feeling happier in just one week...effective, bite-sized pieces that fit into your busy schedule."

> — **Lisa Ferrer**, International Grand Master Teacher & Intuitive Healer

"This is a gem of a book that will provide you with rewards and inspiration for years to come!"

> — **Jennifer Anderson, PCC,** author of the bestselling book, Plant Yourself Where You Will Bloom

"Brain Makeover *is perfect and timely for the times we live in. Phyllis Ginsberg has taken key concepts like happiness, positive mindset, the need for play and me-time and created simple and practical tools to help us experience them in our everyday life. I particularly love the Weekly Messages which are short, doable and interesting to integrate into our daily routine. Wise, practical and chockfull of ideas,* Brain Makeover *will help you live a life of joy, purpose, and meaning.*"

> — **Uma Girish**, *Grief Guide, author of Hay House transformational memoir* Losing Amma, Finding Home: A Memoir About Love, Loss and Life's Detours

"Brain Makeover *is ideal for individuals who have tried and tried to achieve happiness and health in their lives but haven't succeeded. This book can guide you step by step to achieve your goals. As a fellow health professional, I know that it isn't a "quick fix" – and Phyllis knows that too! Be patient with yourself and let this book this book help guide you!*"

> — **Susie Garcia, RDN**, *author of* Psyched to be Skinny

"Once you learn how your brain works it all makes sense. Phyllis' weekly messages will help to transform your physical and emotional stress to a new level of calm and happiness with practical practices that are easy to implement and are very user-friendly!"
> — **Debbie Katz**, *MFT*

Fan Mail from Brain Makeover Readers

Hi Phyllis,

I am love, love, loving your book! Read it cover to cover over the weekend, and we've implemented week 1 at home. Each night my husband, and I talk about our 5 happy things, and I have definitely noticed how that changes our entire dinner conversation and our attitudes for the rest of the evening. Complaining about the things that didn't go well during the day just doesn't seem to fit. Thank you again for coming into our lives and for sharing your wonderful work.
– A.W.

Dear Phyllis,

You don't know me, but your dad brought me a copy of your book saying I would probably enjoy it…he did, and I do! I will probably finish reading it tonight and will purchase copies for myself and to give to my son and daughters.
Sincerely,
– F.A.

Hi Phyllis,
I am on Week 4 and loving the transformation.
Thanks Phyllis,
– T.O.

Hi Phyllis, I purchased your book and gave it away on New Year's Day. I had dinner that evening with my Mom & Dad who just turned 90. I thought I would bring the book and do the 1st week together. My Dad loved the book and couldn't put it down, so I gave it to him. Now... I'll need to purchase another one!
– S.M.

Hi Phyllis,
I am enjoying Brain Makeover. *I bought a journal yesterday to record my daily joyful experiences. Diving right in!*
Thanks again,
– J.P.

Hi Phyllis,
Your Brain Makeover *tips are definitely helping me to relieve and release those pressure thoughts away and allow a much more restful sleep.*
Take care!
– L.M.

Hi Phyllis,
What is the power of one voice; how does that voice reach people for the good. Too many times in life most people only can hear the hurt voice, angry voice or selfish voice. As you know negative thoughts can sometimes dominate a day. One voice that strives to be good and thoughtful, endeavors to bring joy and love, fights to be heard over the mind of negatives. Thank you for being that voice in my life right now through Brain Makeover.
It means a lot.
– A.C.

Brain
Makeover

A WEEKLY GUIDE TO A HAPPIER,
HEALTHIER AND MORE ABUNDANT LIFE

Phyllis Ginsberg

Finesse
Walnut Creek, CA

Finesse
2950 Buskirk Ave., Suite 150
Walnut Creek, CA 94597
www.phyllisginsberg.com

Ordering Information:
Quantity sales. Special discounts are available on quantity purchases by corporations, associations, and others. For details, contact the "Special Sales Department" at the address above.

Medical Disclaimer:
The content in this book is for information purposes only and not offered as medical or psychological advice, guidance or treatment. This book is not intended as a substitute for medical advice, diagnosis or treatment. The reader should regularly consult a physician in matters relating to his/her health, particularly with respect to any symptoms that may require diagnosis or medical attention. Please see a medical or mental health professional if you need help with depression, illness or have any concerns whatsoever.

Brain Makeover/ Phyllis Ginsberg. —2nd ed.
ISBN 978-1-7336939-4-3

Contents

*Brain Makeover is dedicated to my late Uncle Gil.
His death in 2013 inspired me to live more fully
and on purpose.*

An Invitation for You

I invite you to contact me with your questions, comments, progress or challenges as you put Brain Makeover *into action.*

Website: www.phyllisginsberg.com

Email: phyllis@phyllisginsberg.com

Facebook: www.facebook.com/phyllis.ginsberg

I look forward to hearing from YOU!

Need a Keynote Speaker, or someone for Breakout Sessions, Workshops, or Retreats? Contact me by email.

As you read this book and benefit from it, please consider leaving a positive review on Amazon so others may find this book and benefit as well. If there was anything you think should be changed, please email me.

Introduction

In 2005, I was in near burnout in every area of my life. I had no idea of the journey I would be embarking on when I took time off from work. I didn't set out to give myself a "brain makeover," but that's the best way I can describe it. It's like I was put in the situation where I couldn't live my life in the same way, and I had to make some new decisions, or I would end up with some serious health problems.

I don't know how I did it, working 12-14 hours a day as a Child Custody Evaluator with a full therapy private practice, and an eight-month waiting list. There was no end in sight to the amount of work I had. I put my health in jeopardy while my family got less and less of me. My daughters were growing up fast and would soon be off to college, and I yearned to spend more time with them. My husband was supportive of my work and encouraged me to start a waiting list rather than turn down clients. I felt like a machine, churning out work without much personal satisfaction.

I recognized the old pattern that was driving my life, "doing what I was supposed to do." My belief that I could do anything was being challenged. The need for financial security and saving for retirement played a big role. I earned great money and was in high demand by judges and attorneys because of the quality of my work. I got caught up in it all and couldn't sustain it, because as a human being I lost the "being" part of me. I became a human doing, cut off from my feelings, needs, and wants.

I remember the day I decided to take a year off from work. Within a month I had referred my clients to other therapists and notified the courts. It wasn't until I stopped working that I felt the full impact of all the stress I was holding. I couldn't function at high speed anymore. I was forced to slow down. For the first time in my life, I felt like I needed to be taken care of. Fortunately, my husband and daughters were supportive and gave me plenty of time and space to "be" and figure out what was next.

I couldn't go back to being who I was, nor did I want to. This experience was a journey of me discovering who I was, who I wanted to become, and how to make it happen. I learned to put my focus on happiness, I used EFT Tapping to process emotions and rewire my brain, and I practiced being different, on purpose.

I was in the pursuit of how to live MY life.

It wasn't always fun or easy, but I was committed to using the tools I learned in my training as a therapist and beyond. I immersed myself in Positive Psychology and brain research and created a way of using Tapping that acknowledged how I was feeling, what else was possible, then anchored in something new.

My thoughts were shifting as I kept a Happiness Journal. (See What's Your Happiest Moment of The Day? on page 1.) No longer were my days filled with what was wrong. I now had something positive to focus on – looking for my happiest moments of the day. I also started doing things I enjoyed, connecting with friends and a lot of reading and writing.

What changed for me was that I got to know myself on a deeper level. I let go of some key thoughts, beliefs, and patterns that were driving my behaviors. It was a process of, for the first time in my life, honoring me and not putting everyone else first. I let go of the fear, worry, and anxiety about having to be strong for everyone as I wondered why they got to do what they wanted, and I couldn't. What right did they have that I didn't?

As I questioned my beliefs, I realized I could change them. I could rewrite the rules.

I didn't set out to write this book when I began writing a blog. Each week, on Mondays, I wrote about Healthy Mind, as I was going through my transformation. I've never been one to share my struggles, even with those closest to me. It was scary to be public about what was going on with me, but I didn't want to continue suffering and doing it alone. Perhaps you can relate to having to be strong, keeping it together and marching on. It's how most of us were raised in my generation.

There is a better way, and I can't wait for you to get started. *Brain Makeover* is a book I wish I had when I was in my teens and early adulthood. Simple, practical, and easy-to-do activities at the end of each weekly reading will have you feeling happier, healthier, and more abundant as you shift out of survival thinking and into what is possible for you!

You Can Change Your Brain

You may have picked up this book to help you shift the way you feel, physically or emotionally. Since our thoughts affect our health, and you can change your thoughts, it's possible to improve your health and happiness.

The brain and the way it thinks is the cause of anxiety and stress. Anxiety disorders are thought disorders, which means that with the messages and tools in this book, you will easily be able to turn around your experience from anxiety and stress to health and happiness!

- According to the National Institute of Mental Health, over 19% of all adults (age 18 and older) in the United States have an anxiety disorder in any given year. That's 40 million people!

- In the US, the prevalence of obesity among adults, according to the American Heart Association, increased from 1999 to 2000 through 2013 to 2014 from 30.5% to 37.7%.

- The Center for Disease Control and Prevention reports that about 70 million Americans suffer from chronic sleep problems.

Night-time worrying about day-time troubles is a serious cause of sleep problems. Stressful thoughts create the production of stress hormones, including cortisol, which has been shown to make it difficult to lose weight and easy to gain weight — just the opposite of what we want.

The Evolution of Thought

As humans, from our previous need to survive in the wild, we have been programmed to think in ways that will protect us from harm. As children, we develop coping skills to keep us safe. We also adopt beliefs to keep us safe. Your brain goes on alert looking to deliver what you are thinking, even if you are not consciously aware of your thoughts!

Our modern-day fears look different from that of our ancestors'.

Common fears today may include:

1. Fear of judgment or criticism for being different.

2. Fear of not being good enough.

3. Fear of lack of money, work, or time.

These fearful thoughts are mostly unconscious and might be running your life. It's no wonder we have a high rate of disease.

Living in FEAR is no longer serving us! Fearful thinking has been the cause of worry and stress that has produced record numbers of people suffering from an array of diseases. Fearful thinking has also prevented us from connecting and experiencing the closeness and connection we so richly deserve. This fear-based thinking we have been programmed with for survival is what is getting in the way of living a happier, healthier, and more prosperous life.

There is a better way! For the first time in human history, we are stepping into "living" life, not just "surviving" life. More and more people are creating the life of their dreams. Brain research, Positive Psychology and the Law of Attraction teach us that we can alter our lives with the power of our thoughts.

The field of Epigenetics has shown that how we think impacts the environment of our genes – which ones get turned on and which ones remain dormant. Fear, worry, and stress produce stress hormones that can have a negative impact on both physical and mental health. Happy, calm, and peaceful thoughts and feelings create an environment of feel-good hormones that allow for greater health and healing.

What You Can Expect

Brain Makeover will have you thinking differently as you engage with the weekly readings and put them into action! Through fun activities and thought-provoking wisdom, you will naturally experience how the power of your mind influences your life to become happier, healthier, and more abundant!

Brain Makeover draws upon the information from the exciting field of Positive Psychology, the study of happiness, and the latest research into the brain, including how to build new neural pathways. Each week you will find practical and easy-to-follow messages packed full of inspiring information and tools to use throughout the year.

As you apply *Brain Makeover,* you can expect to see changes in the following three areas:

Thoughts: Scientists believe we have 60,000 thoughts a day! Your brain searches for what you think about, and these thoughts determine whether you will feel stressed or happy. It's crucial that you cast your thinking in the direction of better feeling thoughts; *Brain Makeover* will guide you to do that.

Habits: Your brain functions mostly on autopilot. Research has shown that we tend to think the same 95% of thoughts over and over each day, and 80% of these repetitive thoughts are negative! Your brain is hard-wired for survival. What in the past has served you well to survive may be the very cause of your struggles today. This book will have you more conscious of your thoughts and change your habits to ones that lead to greater happiness, health, and abundance.

Enjoyment: Play is a necessary component of a happy life. Studies show that play deprivation affects every area of your life, and yet it's easy nowadays to forget the importance of fun, play, and enjoyment. *Brain Makeover* weaves play throughout its pages as a reminder of the foundation for a happy, healthy life.

Brain Makeover has been expanded for a more personal experience. Insight and awareness about YOU will make it easier to become happier, healthier, and more abundant!

At the end of each short weekly reading, you'll find specific activities designed for that week. *Brain Makeover* is now a book you can use daily, to become aware of your thoughts, to shift out of survival thinking, and to connect more easily with yourself and others.

You'll find everything you need within the pages of this book, including space for you to write in. It doesn't have to take a long time or be difficult as you take the time to get to know you and your inner workings better. Once you identify patterns and habits that are not working for you any longer, you can choose to replace them with something better.

This second edition of Brain Makeover has a section on the Emotional Freedom Technique or EFT Tapping. It was mentioned in the first edition, and with it becoming more mainstream, I felt it was time to include specifics, so you too can benefit from the results so many people are experiencing. If you're not familiar with EFT Tapping, it frees stored emotions in the body by tapping on meridian points, similar to acupuncture. This modality is the most effective tool I know of to quickly reduce anxiety, stress, overwhelm, fear, and in some cases, pain. You'll find several pages of information on this technique and how to use it in Week 20, Navigating the World of Emotions (on page 79).

Brain Makeover was written for you to keep each topic at the forefront of your mind for a week. By thinking about the weekly topics, and taking action, you'll be building new neural pathways that will boost your happiness to higher levels! Each week has questions to consider or actions to take that will guide you to different ways of thinking about and looking at situations.

As you read the following pages, you may find yourself relating to the same challenges I faced because of my survival thinking. I chose to become happier and healthier and you can too!

What are you waiting for? It's time to deliberately design your life. The life that you are destined to "LIVE." Give yourself permission to do what you love, be who you are, and live a life that brings you joy.

Have fun with it!

Phyllis Ginsberg

Ways to Use Brain Makeover

Here are some tips to get the most out of *Brain Makeover*:

1.   Start by taking the **Brain Makeover Beginning Assessment** (on page xxv). Then begin the weekly readings with week one and focus on each topic for seven days by reading the passage daily and doing the practice for that week.

If you're like many people who read self-help books, you read them, get a few gems, keep reading, and never put what you read into action. If you want a different result, you must "do" something different. When you see a suggestion, and you'd like to incorporate it into your life, do it within 24 hours. You're more likely to do it and gain the benefit if you start while it's fresh in your mind.

2.   This book was written to follow the Gregorian calendar (used by the United States), with consideration to seasons, weather, and holidays. For example, Week 52 is Brain Compatible New Year's Resolutions. You could focus on this reading at any time of the year that you want a new beginning. You could start reading this book any time of the year either by starting at the beginning or starting with the week that lines up with the calendar.

3.   While reading *Brain Makeover*, you may want to focus on one reading for more than a week to begin to form it into a habit. Be sure after a few weeks to move on to the next reading to continue to reap the rewards of the book.

4.   Read *Brain Makeover* with a friend or family member. Do the activities together, talk about the readings, and support each other as you have fun developing new habits of thoughts and actions.

5.   If you have a specific area you want to work on improving; Thoughts, Feelings, Giving and Receiving, Your Relationship with Yourself, or Fun, Play and Enjoyment, see the index at the back of the book for the readings in each category.

Brain Makeover Beginning Assessment

Personal reflection is a gift you can give yourself so that you aren't running on autopilot, living the same story every day. It allows you to use your awareness to make conscious decisions to design your life for greater health and happiness.

Rate the following statements on a scale of 1-5.

A. My current level of overall satisfaction is (circle one)

1	2	3	4	5
none	low	moderate	elevated	high

B. My current level of overall happiness is (circle one)

1	2	3	4	5
none	low	moderate	elevated	high

C. My current level of overall stress is (circle one)

1	2	3	4	5
none	low	moderate	elevated	high

D. My current level of overall fear is (circle one)

1	2	3	4	5
none	low	moderate	elevated	high

E. When I think about my health, I feel (circle one)

1	2	3	4	5
fear	concern	neutral	good	happy

F. When I think about my finances, I feel (circle one)

1	2	3	4	5
fear	concern	neutral	good	happy

G. When I think about my relationships, I feel (circle one)

1	2	3	4	5
fear	concern	neutral	good	happy

The top three things I worry about are:

1. _____

2. _____

3. _____

In the reading, Reflections of the Year - Week 51 (on page 216), you will have an opportunity to take the Brain Makeover Follow-Up Assessment to measure your progress.

What's Your Happiest Moment of the Day?

What makes you happy? Do you ever stop to identify what makes you happy and anchor in the feeling? Some of the benefits of focusing on what makes you happy are feeling better about yourself, an improved sense of well-being, and feeling more content. When you acknowledge and embrace your happiness, life seems to flow better.

I invite you to commit to keeping a Happiness Journal. I suggest you do this every night, even if it takes a little effort. A new habit can take time to develop but will be worth it!

In your Happiness Journal, write three to five of your happiest moments of the day just before going to sleep.

It could look like one of mine.

The happiest moments of my day were:

1. Feeling the sunshine on my face.
2. Seeing the orange poppy flowers on my drive to work.
3. Spending 10 minutes working on my jigsaw puzzle.
4. Walking with a friend at lunch.
5. Watching my favorite TV show.

Focus on your happiness and watch it expand!

For the next seven days, write your happiest moments of the day here:

Day 1

1. _____
2. _____
3. _____
4. _____
5. _____

Day 2

1. _____
2. _____
3. _____
4. _____
5. _____

Day 3

1. _____
2. _____
3. _____

4. _____

5. _____

Day 4

1. _____

2. _____

3. _____

4. _____

5. _____

Day 5

1. _____

2. _____

3. _____

4. _____

5. _____

Day 6

1. _____

2. _____

3. _____

4. _____

5. _____

Day 7

1. _____

2. _____

3. _____

4. _____

5. _____

What did you notice within yourself as you focused on happiness throughout the week? How did you feel when you laid your head down to sleep? You may want to continue keeping a Happiness Journal in a separate notebook as you move on to the next weekly reading.

_____

_____

_____

_____

_____

_____

_____

_____

_____

_____

_____

_____

_____

_____

_____

_____

_____

It Only Takes 18 Seconds to Change Your Brain

When you rehearse, imagine, or talk to yourself about something either positive or negative, for just 18 seconds, it gets stored in your long-term memory.

How easy is it to focus on an illness, mistakes, past experiences that did not go well, failures, and what you don't like? Many of us get caught up in worry, doubt, and negative self-talk.

How foreign is it to focus on appreciation, gratitude, positive experiences, successes, and self-praise, let alone do it for 18 seconds?

Recent research has validated that what we put our attention on is what shows up. It's like you send out a thought, and there is a field of energy that lines up with that same energy pattern to deliver more of what you think about. The more aware you are about what you think about, the more you will be able to have what you truly want by getting your brain on board.

If you want something different, imagine it! Here are a few examples:

1. To have a healthier body, appreciate the parts of your body that function well. Then imagine your whole body being healthier.

2. To improve a relationship, focus on the parts of it that are satisfying. Then imagine other parts of the relationship functioning as well.

3. To have more abundance in your life, focus on what you already have, and on what is working. Then imagine what it would feel like to have what you desire.

Pay attention to what you pay attention to. Dwell on what you want and what you have that is working, for 18 seconds. It will change your brain!

Take a moment each day to appreciate what you already have that is working, then imagine something you desire, for 18 seconds. Do this each day for a week. Fill in the blank with what you imagine.

Day 1 – I imagined _____

Day 2 – I imagined _____

Day 3 – I imagined _____

Day 4 – I imagined _____

Day 5 – I imagined _____

Day 6 – I imagined _____

Day 7 – I imagined _____

What did you discover by spending 18 seconds each day imagining something that you desire? Do you feel more hopeful about what you want? After focusing on something you appreciate each day, has it become easier to focus on appreciation, gratitude, positive experiences, and successes? Now that you are more aware, has your self-talk shifted to become more positive?

_____

_____

_____

_____

_____

_____

_____

_____

_____

_____

_____

_____

_____

_____

_____

_____
_____
_____
_____
_____
_____
_____
_____
_____
_____
_____
_____
_____
_____
_____
_____
_____
_____
_____
_____
_____
_____
_____
_____
_____
_____

Play Isn't Just for Kids

Research from the University of Houston has shown a direct correlation between play and how much joy and fulfillment people experience in their lives. Play deprivation, like sleep deprivation, negatively affects your well-being, happiness, finances, relationships, and creativity.

What is play? Play is doing something for the pure enjoyment of it, not to win or for any result. Play often puts you in a state of flow, increasing relaxation, decreasing stress, and elevating mood. Play can be done alone or with others. Additional benefits of play include increasing your imagination and bonding with others.

"I'm too busy." "Play is for kids." "Play is frivolous." These are some of the things I heard adults say about play while at a workshop I gave for a company.

If you were brought up with the motto, "Work before play," it can be hard to take time to play, since work never ends and there is always something on the "To-Do List." You may also be self-conscious about letting loose and playing.

But remember, play is essential to living a balanced life.

Find things you like to do. How about playing a game of cards, a musical instrument, or a sport like golf or tennis? Play can be singing or dancing at home alone or with others at karaoke or a party. It can be painting or coloring, or other forms of art. Play can be anything you have fun doing for the pure enjoyment of it!

Take time to play this week, even if it's for just a few minutes. Do things you enjoy, just for the fun of it. Fill in the blank with what you did each day that you played.

Day 1 – Today I _____

Day 2 – Today I _____

Day 3 – Today I _____

Day 4 – Today I _____

Day 5 – Today I _____

Day 6 – Today I _____

Day 7 – Today I _____

How was it to play this week? What did you like best about playing? What did you like least? What were your barriers to play? What do you tell yourself about playing? Where did that belief come from and

how has that belief impacted your life? What commitment can you
make to take time for play?

_____

_____

_____

_____

_____

_____

_____

_____

_____

_____

_____

_____

_____

_____

_____

_____

_____

_____

_____

_____

_____

_____

_____

_____

_____

Moment by Moment

"I have everything I need at this very moment." This is one of my favorite statements I say to myself when I'm feeling overwhelmed, worrying about the future, or caught up about something in the past. That does not mean I don't make plans, set goals, or make "To-Do" lists.

A client shared this story with me about the impact of her mindset shift.

Last year after reading the first edition of Brain Makeover, *I realized how much I was immersed in "not enough" thinking. It permeated just about every area of my life. Being immersed in "not enough" meant that I was constantly stressing about my life and worried. I created never-ending stories about the bad things that were going to happen in the future. I had no energy for my business. I had no faith in possibility. Sometimes I would wake up in the middle of the night in a panic, my heart racing, my mind spinning. I lay in bed reviewing the same old thoughts over and over – I won't have enough for that bill, I might lose my house, what if my husband can't work... There were endless ways "not enough" showed up and I spent many sleepless nights.*

I decided to shift this pattern by becoming vigilant about my thoughts and tune in moment by moment as Phyllis suggested. It took a while to get into a new pattern, but I shifted it. Every time I noticed a negative thought come up, I stopped and asked myself, "Do I have everything I need at this moment?" The answer was almost always Yes! I have everything I need not only to survive, but to thrive. I shifted my focus away from money issues and recognized all the abundance in my life beyond money – I have good friends, I have a beautiful garden, I have family, I have creativity, I have beauty, I have love and so much more. Somehow, I also have just enough money to pay my bills every month and stay solvent. All it took was becoming aware moment by moment how true that was. My worry stories were always no more than speculation.

When you think about it, what do you really need? Saying, "I have everything I need at this very moment," at a core level is true. It's a mindset that can produce a sense of well-being by lowering stress, anxiety, fear, anger, and resentment. You may need to pay a bill next week, deal with a difficult person at work, or are worried about retiring. And, at this very moment, you are okay and have everything you need for right now.

As long as your basic needs are met each day, you truly have everything you need at this moment. Many of us are fortunate to have much more than our basic needs. We may have a computer or smartphone to access knowledge, a job to earn money, a car to get around, good friends or family who love us, or a pet we are fond of.

We may also have a body that functions well most days, allowing us to do all that we do.

Have you noticed throughout your life that most things work out? How many meals have you missed or nights have you not had a place to sleep? When we have the experience that everything we need is here, at this very moment, we can relax.

When you are feeling stressed, for whatever reason, take a minute to feel that, at this very moment, you have everything you need and you are okay. Take a deep breath. Can you feel the serenity?

I've noticed that the more I live from the place of "all is well at this moment," the more all is well in every moment.

Remind yourself daily, for the next week, that all is well at this moment. When you're feeling stressed or lacking something, you can use the statement, "I have everything I need at this very moment." It might be helpful to write the statement on a piece of paper and put it where you can see it daily. Put a check mark next to each day you tell yourself "all is well at this moment."

_____ Day 1   _____ Day 4   _____ Day 7

_____ Day 2   _____ Day 5

_____ Day 3   _____ Day 6

How did it feel to remind yourself "all is well at this moment?" What specifically did you notice about your thoughts? Did you notice your body feel calmer and more relaxed?

_____

_____

_____

_____

_____

_____

_____

_____

_____

_____

_____

_____

_____

_____

_____

_____

_____

_____

_____

_____

_____

_____

Choices, Choices, Choices!

When you don't want to do something, do you ever want to ask, "Do I have to?" What if you don't want to do something like go to work, finish that project, clean house, cook, or exercise? You always have the choice to do or not do _____ (fill in the blank), as long as you are willing to live with the consequences.

Your life is made up of the choices you make. Every moment you are choosing to do something rather than something else. Most of your choices are habitual. While you may not like what you are doing, you very well may like the result. This could be earning a paycheck from working, waking up to a clean kitchen by cleaning it after dinner or feeling fit by getting regular physical activity.

Choose one thing today that you can do, even though you don't enjoy doing it, but you like the results. Focus on the benefits of your choice. You may feel differently about the task and actually find enjoyment in the activity!

Identify one thing you don't like to do and fill it in the blanks for each day. Then, on a scale of 1-10, 1 = not willing, and 10 = very willing, for the next seven days rate your willingness to do what you don't like to do.

Example: I don't like to floss my teeth, but I like the benefits of it, so I willingly choose to floss my teeth. Rating (1-10) _____

Day 1

I don't like to _____,

but I like the benefits of it, so I willingly choose to _____

_____ Rating (1-10) _____

Day 2

I don't like to _____,

but I like the benefits of it, so I willingly choose to _____

_____ Rating (1-10) _____

Day 3

I don't like to _____,

but I like the benefits of it, so I willingly choose to _____

_____ Rating (1-10) _____

Day 4

I don't like to _____,

but I like the benefits of it, so I willingly choose to _____

_____ Rating (1-10) _____

Day 5

I don't like to _____,

but I like the benefits of it, so I willingly choose to _____

_____ Rating (1-10) _____

Day 6

I don't like to _____,

but I like the benefits of it, so I willingly choose to _____

_____ Rating (1-10) _____

Day 7

I don't like to _____,

but I like the benefits of it, so I willingly choose to _____

_____ Rating (1-10) _____

As the week went on, did it become easier to choose to do the activity you started with? What did you learn? What implications might this have for other things you don't like to do?

_____

_____

_____

_____

_____

_____

_____

_____

The Gift of Time

Any time of year is a good time to give the gift of sharing yourself with another person. Time is one of our most precious commodities, and the connection between two people can be priceless. Connecting with others can be enjoyable, and it's good for your health too.

We can "gift" our time with a card or "homemade" gift certificate. Gift your time to someone on their birthday, for a holiday gift, to celebrate an accomplishment, or just because!

Get creative and start thinking of what you enjoy doing with others, be it your partner, children, grandchildren, parents, brothers or sisters, aunts, uncles, grandparents, or friends.

When my kids were little, one of the sweetest presents I received was a booklet of coupons they made for me with gifts of their time.

Here are some ideas to get you started:

- Two hours together, however you would like to spend it

- Going for a walk together

- Giving a hand or foot massage

- Reading a story or book to a child, adult, or senior

- Having coffee or tea together

- Cooking together

- Time to play cards or a game together

When you don't know what to give someone, give the gift of your time!

This week, think of seven ways you can "gift" your time to people you'd like to spend time with or as a way of celebrating something special. Then make it happen. Each day, fill in the blanks with the activity you will do and who you will do it with. Once it's scheduled, place a check mark to show it's calendared.

Day 1
I can gift my time by doing _____
(activity) with _____ (who). _____ It's scheduled.

Day 2
I can gift my time by doing _____
(activity) with _____ (who). _____ It's scheduled.

Day 3

I can gift my time by doing _____

(activity) with _____ (who). _____ It's scheduled.

Day 4

I can gift my time by doing _____

(activity) with _____ (who). _____ It's scheduled.

Day 5

I can gift my time by doing _____

(activity) with _____ (who). _____ It's scheduled.

Day 6

I can gift my time by doing _____

(activity) with _____ (who). _____ It's scheduled.

Day 7

I can gift my time by doing _____

(activity) with _____ (who). _____ It's scheduled.

How did it feel to plan gifts of your time? Was it easy or difficult to come up with activities to do and who to do them with? If it was difficult, what would make it easier?

_____

_____

_____

_____

The Brain Simply Believes...

Your brain is like a computer. "The brain simply believes what you tell it most. And what you tell it about, it will create. It has no choice." This quote was stated at a training I attended on brain research. Did you know that we talk to ourselves at 200-400 words per minute? That's a lot of chatter that we are not aware of.

Awareness is like finding gold! Once you know your "programming" and what you mostly tell yourself, then you can decide if you want to keep it or upgrade it by changing your self-talk. Experts in brain research say, "If you want things to be different you have to do things on purpose." And I say, "If you want something to be different, you must do something different on purpose."

Set aside some time this week to write about the seven questions below. They will help you identify your beliefs and what you mostly tell yourself.

Day 1. Is it possible to really feel happy? Why or why not?

Day 2. Do I believe I have a choice in any situation? Why or why not?

Day 3. Do I criticize myself when I eat something I enjoy that is not healthy? If that's true, what do I tell myself?

Day 4. Am I consumed with worry and stress about the future or anger and resentment about the past? If so, what is preventing me from living in the present.

Day 5. Do I talk to myself as if I were my best friend or worst enemy? What impact does that have on me and my life?

Day 6. Do I believe that it is safer to stuff my feelings or hide them, rather than feel and express them? If yes, what do I do, and when do I stuff or avoid my feelings?

Day 7. Do I tell myself there isn't enough? Isn't enough time, money, resources, or help? In what areas of my life do I tell myself there's not enough and how does that impact me?

What we tell ourselves matters. Shift your self-talk to be more positive and forgiving and see how your life changes!

_____

_____

_____

_____

_____

_____

_____

_____

_____

Allow Others to Give

Do you dare ask for something? Is it easier for you to give than to receive? Do you allow others to give to you and do for you? Is there a part of you that believes that you must do it all on your own? Or thinks that if you receive from someone, then you will owe them something in return? Do you believe you aren't worthy of receiving?

If I asked you to do a small favor for me, what's the first thought that comes to your mind? It's been my experience that if I just ask, most people say, "yes." It wasn't always that way. In fact, I was so used to doing most everything myself, that it didn't occur to me to ask. It wasn't until I was stressed out and overwhelmed that I started asking for simple things like a glass of water or a napkin. I was surprised how easy it was once I got over my thought that I was inconveniencing my husband or my daughters.

Over the years, I got more comfortable asking for help with cooking, doing dishes, laundry, and household chores. I feel less stress on me because I'm not doing it all, and it has brought me closer to the people I ask. The mutual giving and receiving feels much better than before I took the risk to ask. You may feel vulnerable asking, and in some situations, it may require giving up control of being the giver.

Giving and receiving go together; you can't have one without the other. To receive, someone has to give. If you don't allow others to be giving, you block the possibility of receiving, and you cheat others out of the opportunity of giving.

You may not get everything you ask for, but if you don't ask, you will never know the answer. And when someone offers to do something for you, it may feel awkward at first, but with practice, saying "yes" will become more comfortable.

This week, practice receiving by asking for help with the dishes, laundry, housework, a task at work, or ask for a glass of water or anything you would like someone else to do. And when someone offers to do or give you something, practice accepting it and saying, "thank you."

Fill in the blank with what you received next to each day you receive something by asking for it, or it is offered to you.

Day 1 – I received _____

Day 2 – I received _____

Day 3 – I received _____

Day 4 – I received _____

Day 5 – I received _____

Day 6 – I received _____

Day 7 – I received _____

How was it to receive? Did it get easier as the week went on? What impact did it have on your relationship with the people you received from? Did it change your level of stress or happiness? If yes, how so? What will you do differently as a result of this experience?

_____

_____

_____

_____

_____

_____

_____

_____

_____

_____

_____

_____

_____

_____

_____

_____

Make Space for Something New

I often will say that I feel "out of sorts" when I look at the kitchen counter with papers and other items spread out all over it. Once I clear it off, I feel calmer and more focused. It makes me happy to have that space cleared.

Did you know that a cluttered workspace, room, or home has an adverse effect on your emotional well-being? We all have old clothes, kitchen items, and other belongings that we don't use or need anymore but keep.

Clear out a drawer, closet, or space and see what "treasures" you find. Keep what has meaning or is useful and say goodbye to those items that were from a different time in your life and no longer have the same meaning or usefulness. Give away, donate, sell, recycle, or throw out anything you don't have a use for.

Clearing out unnecessary items will have you feeling better about your space and yourself. It also makes space for new beginnings or new opportunities.

Fill in the blank with what items you release next to each day that you clear out a drawer, closet, or area in your home.

Day 1 – Today I _____

Day 2 – Today I _____

Day 3 – Today I _____

Day 4 – Today I _____

Day 5 – Today I _____

Day 6 – Today I _____

Day 7 – Today I _____

How do you feel about your space and yourself after taking steps this week to let go of unnecessary items? Were you surprised by what you were able to accomplish? How might this experience help you to keep a more organized home?

_____

_____

_____

_____

_____

_____

_____

_____

_____

_____

_____

_____

_____

_____

_____

_____

_____

_____

_____

_____

_____

_____

_____

_____

_____

Put Yourself on Your "To-Do" List

It's interesting how difficult it can be to take good care of ourselves. Below are some ideas and ways to put yourself on your "to-do" list every day. Find what works best for you to relax, stimulate your mind, tune into your creativity and just have fun! Try something new. It's for YOU!

READ * TAKE A BATH * GO FOR A WALK * GET A MASSAGE * TAKE UP A HOBBY * SEW * VISIT THE LIBRARY * GARDEN * DO A PUZZLE * MAKE A PHOTO ALBUM * TAKE A NAP * CALL A FRIEND * GO ROLLER SKATING * HAVE A PICNIC * GO DANCING * JOG * GET A FACIAL * SEE A MOVIE * GO SWIMMING * MEDITATE * LEARN TO PLAY AN INSTRUMENT * GO FOR A BIKE RIDE * PLAY WITH CLAY * COLOR WITH CRAYONS * GET A MANICURE OR PEDICURE * SEE A PLAY * BUY SOMETHING NEW * DO CREATIVE WRITING * TAKE A DANCE CLASS * GET AWAY FOR A WEEKEND * COOK SOMETHING NEW * LOOK AT OLD PICTURES * LEARN A NEW LANGUAGE * GO SAILING *WRITE A LETTER TO SOMEONE * TAKE A CLASS * JOURNAL YOUR FEELINGS * PAINT * GO TO A CONCERT * CLEAN OUT A DRAWER

*DRAW * GO OUT TO LUNCH * TAKE UP PHOTOGRAPHY * GO TO THE BEACH * LISTEN TO MUSIC * ICE SKATE * TEXT A FRIEND * PLAY A BOARD GAME * WRITE A SHORT STORY * ATTEND A SPORTING EVENT * LISTEN TO A RELAXATION AUDIO * CREATE A NEW RECIPE * SEND A CARD TO A FRIEND * DO YOGA * BUY YOURSELF FLOWERS*

What will you do for yourself today and every day this week? Fill in the blank with what you did next to each day you do something for YOU.

Day 1 – Today I _____

Day 2 – Today I _____

Day 3 – Today I _____

Day 4 – Today I _____

Day 5 – Today I _____

Day 6 – Today I _____

Day 7 – Today I _____

What was it like to put yourself on your to-do list? How did you feel doing something for you each day? What was the impact? How can you commit to doing this more?

What Makes Up
Your Personality?

Are you funny, smart, calm, driven, cautious, or giving? What makes you unique? Do you ever wonder, "Is it okay to be me with my quirkiness?" "Am I too much?" "What if I'm so different...?" Were you brought up to NOT be seen or heard, and to speak only when spoken to? Do you keep your personality hidden?

Encourage yourself and the people you live and work with to be themselves, warts and all! Acknowledge and try to understand your and their likes and dislikes. It will make living and working together a lot easier than trying to change another person to be who you want them to be because you don't like something about them or agree with them.

Here are some suggestions to bring out the true personality in yourself and others:

1. Discover each other's favorite color, entertainment, food, books, movies, music, sports, talents, interests, passions, etc. For a more

in-depth answer, ask, "What is it that you like about _____?" Example, "What is it that you like about the color red?"

2. When faced with a task, ask others how they would handle it. There are many ways to accomplish things. When appropriate, allow others to do things their way, even if it's different from yours. You will learn how others think and may even learn a new way of doing something!

3. Encourage family members to select pictures that have special meaning to them. Talk about what is so special about the photos, then frame them or put them up on a wall or the refrigerator.

Share this reading with others and ask them to do it with you. Here's to your self-expression!

This week get to know more about the people you live and work with. Put a check mark next to each day you learn something new about someone you regularly interact with.

_____ Day 1   _____ Day 4   _____ Day 7

_____ Day 2   _____ Day 5

_____ Day 3   _____ Day 6

How does it feel to get to know the people in your life better? Do you feel closer to them? What did they get to know about you?

Best Friend or Worst Enemy?

We can be our own worst enemy, talking to ourselves in ways that we would never speak to our friends. It's common for people to be harder on themselves than anyone else is. This ingrained, automatic judgment comes from an inner critic that can interfere with your efforts to be happy and healthy, to have satisfying relationships, or to reach your work or financial goals.

Negative self-talk can be changed with some effort and awareness on your part. Here are several ways to go from being your own worst enemy to becoming your own best friend:

1. Make friends with your inner critic. Become aware of what it says to you and when it shows up.

2. When you have critical thoughts, say, "STOP, take two," silently or out loud, then, just like in filming a movie, redo the scene with a positive statement.

3. Use one of the following "Cheerleading Statements" from Dialectical Behavioral Therapy (DBT) to get a better handle on your situation and feelings:

- I have the right to ask for help and emotional support.

- I can be anxious and still deal with this situation.

- I can't control how other people will act toward me or react to me.

- Today I will be calm and confident.

- I may want to please people I care about, but I do not have to do it all the time.

This week pay close attention to your self-talk and use one or more of the suggested ways listed above to become your best friend.

Each day this week, write what you did to become your own best friend.

Day 1

_____

_____

_____

Day 2

_____

_____

_____

Day 3

_____

_____

_____

Day 4

_____

_____

_____

Day 5

_____

_____

_____

Day 6

_____

_____

_____

Day 7

_____

_____

_____

What did you learn about becoming your own best friend? How did you benefit by being kinder to yourself? What will you do differently as a result?

People Who Laugh Together Are Healthier

The average adult has gone from laughing hundreds of times a day as a child, to laughing only about 20 times a day. Laughter is great for your well-being. It has been shown to reduce stress, strengthen your immune system, and even relieve physical pain.

You may remember hearing about Norman Cousins, who developed a recovery program incorporating megadoses of Vitamin C, along with a positive attitude, love, faith, hope, and laughter induced by Marx Brothers films. He reported, "I made the joyous discovery that ten minutes of genuine belly laughter had an anesthetic effect and would give me at least two hours of pain-free sleep,"

Here are some family friendly suggestions to increase the amount of laughter in your life and relationships:

1. Watch funny movies, television shows, or videos. Find old comedies, sitcoms, or cartoons that you watched as a child. Some classics include, *I Love Lucy* and *The Carol Burnett Show*. There's also,

America's Funniest Home Videos, or you can search the web and YouTube for funny animal/pet videos. *

*If watching with children, it is advised that you find and preview for appropriateness, movies, videos, and photos, without the children.

2. Take fun photos of you and others being silly, making funny faces, or doing something funny.

3. Go to the library or a bookstore and look at joke books.

4. Read the comics together, looking closely at the pictures and expressions of the people and animals.

5. Post something funny to look at on the refrigerator.

6. Have each family member seek out something funny to look at daily. It could be a photo, a comic strip, a greeting card, a drawing, or a figurine. Keep it by your bedside or in the bathroom where you can see it first thing in the morning and just before you go to sleep.

Start and end your day looking at something that makes you laugh. Just don't try brushing your teeth while you are laughing, that could make a mess, although it may make for a great photo!

Make laughter part of your day and then fill in the blank with what you laughed about each day.

Day 1 – Today I laughed about _____

Day 2 – Today I laughed about _____

Day 3 – Today I laughed about _____

Day 4 – Today I laughed about _____

Day 5 – Today I laughed about _____

Day 6 – Today I laughed about _____

Day 7 – Today I laughed about _____

What brings out laughter in you? Was it easy to find things to get you laughing? If not, what prevents you from laughing? What can you do to bring more laughter in your life?

_____

_____

_____

_____

_____

_____

_____

_____

_____

_____

_____

_____

Reclaim the Space in Your Head

It may be time to reclaim the space in your head taken up with thoughts of people who have hurt you. How often do you think about someone you resent? If you are harboring anger and resentment toward someone, it may be time to clear out those thoughts.

Forgive others not because they deserve forgiveness, but because you deserve peace. It's not about them. It's not about forgetting what they have done. It's not about agreeing with them. It's about you coming to terms with what happened, letting it go, and reclaiming the space they take up in your head.

This process came to me when I knew I had to forgive my mom for the things she did to me when I was a child. I can picture myself sitting outside on a sunny spring day in 2006, writing each of the steps and feeling the hurt, pain, and sadness. I questioned whether I was ready to let it go. I decided I was. It was a defining moment when I lit fire to the pages in a soup pot in the backyard.

Afterward, I then sat down and for the first time, felt compassion for my mom. I wrote a prayer of what I wanted for her that she couldn't give to me because she didn't have it to give. For the first time in my life, I felt at peace with my mom who died when I was 15. The decades of grief, anger, and resentment that I carried were gone. I was free, and since that day, I've been aspiring to live as I wanted for my mom. That prayer has been the cornerstone of my personal growth and development. I use it in my work with clients and have a big poster of the prayer hanging in my office. One day it will become a book!

I don't know what will happen for you as you use this process, but many people have reported a positive shift in their thoughts about a person or situation.

The following 6-step process can be done privately or with the support of a trusted friend or mental health professional. This process DOES NOT include any interaction with the person you have resentment toward. Don't rush to forgive. Allow for however long you need to complete the process. It can be done over days, weeks, or months

1. Decide that you want peace around a person or event.

2. Write down all the hurtful things you experienced.

3. Write (but DO NOT send) a letter to the person expressing your feelings of anger, resentment, hurt, pain, sadness, etc.

4. Next, write to the person (but DO NOT send) what you needed and didn't get, and how you would have liked it to be.

5. Experience your feelings as you look over all your writings.

6. When you are ready, declare your forgiveness. If you desire, you can symbolize your forgiveness by safely burning your writings, shredding them, or burying them in the ground.

This process can be used to forgive a person, a situation, an entity, or yourself!

This week, start with the first step and each day continue with the steps, doing as much as you are ready for. If you get through the 6-step process, then either choose another person, situation, or yourself to forgive or take the time to notice what changed for you as a result of doing this process.

Fill in the blank with what you did next to each day you do something to reclaim the space in your head or notice what changed after you do the process.

Day 1 – Today I _____

Day 2 – Today I _____

Day 3 – Today I _____

Day 4 – Today I _____

Day 5 – Today I _____

Day 6 – Today I _____

Day 7 – Today I _____

Now that you've started and may have finished the process of reclaiming the space in your head, how does it feel? What has been the most powerful part of the process? What will you do differently, and what support might you need moving forward or to complete the process?

_____

_____

_____

_____

_____

_____

_____

_____

_____

_____

_____

_____

_____

_____

_____

_____

_____

_____

_____
_____
_____
_____
_____
_____
_____
_____
_____
_____
_____
_____
_____
_____
_____
_____
_____
_____
_____
_____
_____
_____
_____
_____
_____
_____
_____
_____

The Risk It Took to Remain Tight Inside the Bud...

"The risk it took to remain tight inside the bud was more painful than the risk it took to blossom." – Anais Nin.

We tend to hang on to what we know, even if we don't like it. Either because we don't know how to be any other way or because we fear the unknown that comes with changing.

Most of us are uncomfortable with change, let alone big change, like blossoming into a beautiful flower or if you prefer, sprouting wings in a cocoon and then breaking free into a butterfly. At a certain point, we all go through events where we find ourselves in a position where it is more painful to stay the way we are than to take the risk to grow.

I had one of those defining moments regarding celebrating my birthday. I took a risk and shared some old buried feelings with some trusted friends. On that day, I wasn't even going to tell them it was my birthday. I took a risk to speak up because it was more painful not to be acknowledged and celebrated on my birthday than it was to speak up.

The amount of support I received was tremendous. I was surprised that anyone would be interested in hearing my story and why I became withdrawn around my birthday. Although it was uncomfortable at the time, it was nowhere as painful as tightly holding on to those feelings alone. I felt a sense of relief by sharing and felt closer to my friends. I knew that a huge shift had taken place, a blossoming! This was the beginning of me taking risks and sharing more of me with others.

Is there an area of your life you are ready to blossom in?

This week, spend some time journaling about one or two areas of your life that you know could be significantly better and what that might look like. Put a check mark next to each day you journal.

_____ Day 1   _____ Day 4   _____ Day 7

_____ Day 2   _____ Day 5

_____ Day 3   _____ Day 6

How was it to identify and write about an area or two of your life that you are dissatisfied with? What steps are you willing to take to improve your situation?

_____

_____

_____

_____

_____

_____

_____

_____

_____

_____

_____

_____

_____

_____

_____

_____

_____

_____

_____

_____

_____

_____

_____

_____

_____

_____

_____

_____

_____

Which Came First, the Chicken or the Egg?

You've heard the question, "Which came first, the chicken or the egg?" Does it really matter? It may not matter when you are talking about chickens and eggs, but it could matter when you are talking about happiness and events.

At one time or another, you've probably said, "I'll be happy when I _____." Fill in the blank with what fits for you: get a new job/promotion, car, wardrobe, get married, have a baby, have a certain amount of money in the bank, lose weight, go on vacation, retire, etc. You get the idea. When you anticipate that a future event will make you happy, it may prevent you from being happy today, right now, at this moment.

Positive Psychology research shows that people who are happier are healthier, make more money, and feel better about themselves. Think about it. When you're feeling happy, you carry yourself differently than when you're not feeling happy. Perhaps you carry your head high, you're more open to new experiences, and it's easier to get along with others.

How could you be happy regardless of your circumstances? Might being happy now allow you to gravitate toward the things you desire by seeing and taking advantage of opportunities that present themselves?

It could be that happiness *is* the way.

Put a check mark next to each day you think about and let happiness lead the way.

_____ Day 1   _____ Day 4   _____ Day 7

_____ Day 2   _____ Day 5

_____ Day 3   _____ Day 6

How was it to let happiness lead the way? What challenges got in the way? Did you notice a difference in how you felt when you were happy, even if your circumstances weren't the best? What will you do going forward to lead with happiness?

_____

_____

_____

_____

_____

What to Say When You Talk to Yourself and Others!

Many adults were not brought up with positive, encouraging comments, but instead, critical negative put-downs. The following statements come from the book, *Predictive Parenting: What to Say When You Talk to Your Kids*, by Shad Helmstetter. While these statements may feel foreign at first, they are worth saying to yourself, your spouse, child, and any other human being!

Positive, encouraging statements can be motivating and smooth out relationships. A client of mine told me this story about positive encouragement in action. Here is how she related the story to me.

> *My husband used to take my forgetting to turn lights off personally. Every time I forgot to turn off the lights, he would yell at me saying "why don't you listen to me and remember to turn the lights off." I would turn red with frustration and embarrassment and then hastily turn off all the lights I left on. I hated getting yelled at, and I also felt bad about leaving the*

lights on, knowing I could do better. Somehow this wasn't motivation enough for me to remember to turn off the lights and it created resentment in our relationship on both sides.

One day, I pushed back, using some tips I got from Phyllis. When my husband yelled at me, I said, "you know it might actually work better if you acknowledge me when I do remember to turn the lights off and maybe I will do it more often." My husband took this advice to heart and started complimenting me when I remembered to turn off the lights. The result is not perfect, but I turn off the lights more often than not, and we are both much happier as a result.

Here are some statements to get you started on using positive, encouraging comments:

That was really great! * You were wonderful! * You really do that well. * You're a winner! * I trust you. * I can always count on you. * You're really smart. * I like the way you did that. * You're really fun to be with. * You really take responsibility for yourself. * I like the way you keep your room neat. * I like that I can rely on you. * Good job! * You're beautiful. * You make every day brighter. * You have a nice smile. * You're a good friend. * You really get along well with other kids. * You're an achiever. * You're very creative. * I've noticed you're a very good listener. * It's obvious that you care about yourself. * You're a good runner. * I'm proud of your schoolwork. * That's much better. * You're doing great! * You're really special. * I love you, and I like you too! * You really practice good manners. * There is no one else like you in the whole world. * You sure are talented! *

If it feels good to read these to yourself, imagine how others will feel hearing them. This week, make someone's day with a positive, uplifting comment like one of these! Put a check mark next to each day you say a statement to someone to validate their greatness or to encourage them.

_____ Day 1   _____ Day 4   _____ Day 7

_____ Day 2   _____ Day 5

_____ Day 3   _____ Day 6

What happened when you started using positive statements with people? How did that change your relationship?

_____

_____

_____

_____

_____

_____

_____

_____

_____

_____

_____

_____

I Think I Can, I Think I Can, I Think I Can

You can train your brain to work for you rather than against you by thinking in the direction of what you want, even if you aren't sure how to get there. If you don't fully believe in yourself, and the most you can say is, "I think I can," that's a great start.

In the classic children's book, *The Little Engine That Could*, that most of us grew up with, the shiny young train didn't think it could make it up the mountain. He used the phrase, "I think I can, I think I can, I think I can," and by the end of the book, he did.

Believing in yourself is a process of expecting and experiencing positive outcomes that build confidence. It helps to have positive expectations when faced with a challenge. Affirm what you want. Tell yourself, "I think I can." Or, "I can do that." And as Dr. Wayne Dyer wrote about in his book titled, *You'll See It When You Believe It*, you too may just find yourself saying, "I thought I could, I thought I could, I thought I could."

What have you been hesitant to do, that with an, "I think I can" outlook, may make it possible?

This week think about something you want and become aware when doubts and fears enter your mind. Remind yourself that it's just your brain trying to keep you safe from the unknown, disappointment, or repeating a past mistake. Acknowledge the thought and any feelings, then when you are ready, begin thinking in the direction of what you want and that it's possible. Tell yourself, "I think I can, I think I can, I think I can," as you imagine your desired outcome.

Put a check mark next to each day you tell yourself, "I think I can, I think I can, I think I can," as you imagine your desired outcome.

_____ Day 1   _____ Day 4   _____ Day 7

_____ Day 2   _____ Day 5

_____ Day 3   _____ Day 6

What did you learn about yourself and your thinking? How can that help you to think in the direction of what you want?

_____

_____

_____

_____

_____

_____

Have You Ever Put Yourself in a Time-Out?

Time-outs are generally thought to be used with children, and they can be beneficial for adults too! The purpose of a time-out is to take a break or a pause from a situation, usually to calm down and then think about what happened and what you want to happen next. When considering to take a time-out, it is respectful to let other people, even your children, know that you are taking a time-out – a break to calm down and think, rather than walk away or storm off.

Just like for children, adult time-outs should be short, about 10-15 minutes. Then check in with the other person. If you are not ready to resume the conversation, then you might propose to table the topic until later that day or the next day, to give yourself time to get clear on what your position is and what you really want to say. A time-out can be effective when you need to think about a consequence for a child, when you are feeling overwhelmed and can't think clearly, when you feel too emotional to make a wise decision, or when you're feeling pressured about a decision that needs to be made.

A time-out can be taken in a quiet room, including the bathroom, or sitting or walking outside. It might be preferable to sit in your car rather than drive if you are feeling emotional. Just make sure you can focus if you go for a drive.

If you interact with children, your own or someone else's, it's great modeling for them to see you use time-outs for yourself as a good thing to regroup your thoughts and feelings, rather than as a consequence.

This week is about learning to pause. Practice taking time-outs for small things this week, so you can know how to use them when you are triggered and need to take a time-out to regroup your thoughts and feelings.

Put a check mark next to each day you take a time-out to take a break from a situation at home or work.

_____ Day 1   _____ Day 4   _____ Day 7

_____ Day 2   _____ Day 5

_____ Day 3   _____ Day 6

What did you learn by taking time-outs this week? How did it impact your relationships with the people you told you were going to take a time-out? What impact did it have on you and were you able to come back to the situations calmer and with more clarity?

_____

_____

_____

_____

_____

_____

_____

_____

_____

_____

_____

_____

_____

_____

_____

_____

_____

_____

_____

_____

_____

_____

_____

_____

Navigating the World of Emotions

Many of us learned to ignore our "negative" emotions due to a cultural belief system that they should be avoided for safety. The reverse is actually true. We are better off when we acknowledge how we are really feeling instead of pretending everything is okay. Honor and embrace your sadness, fear, anger, and disappointment. Feel your feelings and let them pass through. They won't last long if you allow yourself to feel them fully, to discharge the energy they hold. It's important to find safe ways to express your feelings. Unexpressed sadness and anger turned inward can lead to depression.

EFT Tapping

There's a highly effective, easy-to-follow technique I use with clients and teach them to use on themselves called EFT Tapping or the Emotional Freedom Technique. By tapping on various acupressure points, stored emotions are released from the body allowing for quick relief from anxiety, fears, phobias, and stress. For some people, it even reduces physical pain. Brain scans have shown that Tapping calms the amygdala, the part of the brain that responds to stress and signals the fight or flight response by producing stress hormones. Tapping also rewires the brain, creating new neural pathways.

Here's how it works: You will tap on meridian points on your face and body. Use two fingers and tap lightly on each of the tapping points as you say some statements (instructions follow). It's that easy. If you're new to Tapping, you can learn more by watching my Introduction to Tapping video on my website at https://www.phyllisginsberg.com/tapping-with-phyllis.

I invite you to experience Tapping by referring to the Tapping Points Chart that follows and the words in the next paragraph. Try a round of tapping, without any statements, to get familiar with the feel of it.

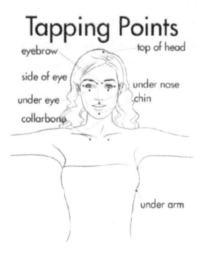

Tapping Points

eyebrow — top of head
side of eye — under nose
under eye — chin
collarbone
under arm

Take two fingers and tap lightly several times on the Eyebrow Point, where your eyebrow starts closest to your nose. Then tap on the Side of the Eye Point. It's on the bone near the eye. Next, tap several times Under Your Eye, on the bone just under the pupil of your eye. Then tap Under Your Nose. Next, tap in the Chin Crease. Then on the Collarbone, tap on either side. Move to Under Arm, about 4 inches from your armpit. And the last tapping point is Top of Head.

Here are the abbreviations for the Tapping Points:

EB (eyebrow)
SE (side of eye)
UE (under eye)
UN (under nose)
CH (chin crease)
CB (collarbone)
UA (under the arm)
TH (top of head)

Before you begin tapping, think about a situation and the emotion you are feeling. Then rate your level of stress or discomfort on a scale of 1 - 10 (1 = no stress or discomfort, 10 = high stress or discomfort). The first round of tapping will be to acknowledge what is true for you; your thoughts and feelings. By tapping and acknowledging what is true for you, it frees the stored emotions in your body.

Here is a sample script to use. Tap on each of the tapping points as you say the statements provided and fill in the blanks or modify the statements to be true for you.

Acknowledging Tapping

EB: I feel _____ (emotion)

SE: I'm thinking about _____ (situation)

UE: I don't like feeling this way.

UN: I feel the stress in my body.

CH: It's in my _____ (body part)

CB: I don't like feeling this way.

UA: It happened; _____ (situation)

TH: I feel so _____ (emotion)

Take a deep breath and notice any thoughts and feelings that came up during the tapping or after.

Rate your level of discomfort again on a scale of 1 - 10. If your level decreased, that's great! If your level increased, that's great too! It means you have gotten in touch with something significant. Rate it on a scale of 1-10 and do another round of tapping saying statements that are true for you; your thoughts and feelings. Then take a big breath and notice how you feel. Rate yourself again to see if your number decreased. Continue tapping until you feel some relief. It may take several rounds. Once your level decreases to a three or below, you can introduce possibilities into your tapping.

You can begin to rewire your brain with Possibility Tapping. Here you will be saying possibility statements as you tap on each of the points.

Possibility Tapping

EB: I wonder what I can do differently.

SE: I wonder how I can think about this in a different way.

UE: I wonder what else is possible.

UN: I wonder how I can look at this situation differently.

CH: If I had a new idea, I wonder what it would be.

CB: Maybe there is a different way of looking at this.

UA: Maybe I don't have to solve it all by myself.

TH: Maybe it's mine to solve.

Take a deep breath.

Notice how you feel and any thoughts you have. Rate your level of discomfort again on a scale of 1 - 10. Did it go down? Did you get clarity about something specific? Possibility Tapping shifts your thinking from problem-focused to solution-focused. You may or may not have gotten an answer or solution but be open to receiving one. Sometimes it comes in a dream or in the shower. These are times when you're not preoccupied and can receive messages.

Tapping is the fastest, safest, and most effective modality I know of to get relief for myself and my clients. To find out more about EFT Tapping and the courses I offer, go to my website at www.phyllisginsberg.com.

Other Safe Ways to Honor and Express Emotions

1. Talk to a trusted friend or mental health professional about how you feel.

2. Journal your thoughts and feelings in a notebook. This would give you good material to do Tapping on.

3. Express your feelings by writing a letter to those who you feel hurt you, but be careful about sending it. Wait a few days before deciding whether to send or share what you wrote. Remember, the purpose of writing is for YOU to feel YOUR feelings.

4. Express your emotions through art: paint, draw, color, use clay, or other forms of artistic expression.

5. Sit quietly and just allow the emotions to pass through you. Be the observer watching you experience your emotions, knowing that they are not you and this will soon pass.

The more you allow yourself to feel emotions as they occur, the freer you will be to feel happiness and joy.

Put a check mark next to each day you do something to honor and express your emotions.

_____ Day 1   _____ Day 4   _____ Day 7

_____ Day 2   _____ Day 5

_____ Day 3   _____ Day 6

What were some of the things you did to honor and express your emotions? What was most effective? What did you notice about your thoughts and feelings? What changed?

_____

_____

_____

_____

_____

_____

What's Under All That Anger?

Anger, with all its intensity, can seem like a primary emotion, but it's actually a secondary emotion. Under the anger, there are always deeper feelings of fear, hurt, or sadness. For some people, feeling angry is an automatic reaction when triggered by an event, something someone said or didn't say, or did or didn't do. You may feel angry at yourself for things you said or did, opportunities you let pass by, etc. It's less vulnerable to say you are feeling angry than to admit that you are feeling sad, scared, or hurt.

When you experience a surge of anger, greater than it ought to be for the situation, it's a clue that it is probably related to an old hurt from your past. Ask yourself: What might I be sad about? Or what might I be scared of? The answer may give you a clue to what's truly going on within you.

Remember, anger is protecting you from some very tender feelings. Be gentle with yourself with whatever comes up. One way to be kind to yourself is to tell yourself what you'd like someone else to tell you, or to ask yourself, "What would I tell a friend who was feeling this way?"

Anger can be scary. As a child, I grew up with a mother who was in chronic pain and angry a lot of the time. I don't believe she had a clue how afraid I was to approach her even when I wanted to share something good. Unknowingly, she scared me, and I missed the opportunity to get closer to her. Because of my mom's anger, I learned to shut down and not express myself, good or bad. It wasn't until years later that I allowed myself to feel my anger, and with that, the hurt and sadness. Now, I welcome my feelings, even anger. I trust that I can work through my feelings and am happier as a result.

This week, journal about times when you've felt angry, hurt, or sad. Be open to understanding the origins of how you feel. As you write, ask yourself: What might I be sad about? Or what might I be scared of? The answer may give you a clue to what's actually going on within you.

Put a check mark next to each day that you take the time to write and become aware of deeper feelings.

_____ Day 1   _____ Day 4   _____ Day 7

_____ Day 2   _____ Day 5

_____ Day 3   _____ Day 6

What did you discover about yourself from journaling about times when you've felt angry, hurt, or sad? What impact does your anger have on others? What will you do differently with what you learned?

_____

_____

_____

_____

_____

_____

_____

_____

_____

_____

_____

_____

_____

_____

_____

_____

_____

_____

_____

_____

_____

_____

_____

The Domino Effect

Have you ever stopped to think about the impact of what you say and do have on others? The effect of what we say and do, good or bad, ripples out beyond ourselves, and even beyond the people we interact with.

A client of mine shared her experience of the domino effect with me.

As I was waiting for my flight at the airport, I witnessed the sweetest exchange between two people. Before this beautiful exchange, I was feeling tired, angry and irritable. My flight was delayed several hours, and all I could think about was being home in my own bed. The more I thought about it, the worse I felt.

I started to question why I chose this airline and why did I choose to travel during the holidays? I didn't want to talk to anybody. I just wanted to be home.

I watched people come off the plane that finally got here and would soon be leaving with me on it to get me home. That's when I saw and heard a woman praising her child for doing so well on the flight. While most people were in a hurry to get on their way, this woman stopped to the side and gave her daughter a big hug. It warmed my heart to watch the brief time it took to validate this little girl.

I boarded my flight with a smile and lightness in my body. No longer was I focused on what I was missing. I even told this story to the person sitting next to me!

When you hear judgmental, condescending, or hurtful words, whether directed at you or another person, it is liable to cause a range of feelings from discomfort to hurt, sadness, or anger. Not only do other people negatively affect you by what they say and do, we too must realize that others are affected by our words and actions.

On the other hand, one random act of kindness, as simple as a smile or a kind word, can cause a domino effect, positively impacting the recipient, which then sets the tone for them to conduct themselves in a positive way, and who knows how many other people will be affected, all because one person decided to spread some kindness.

What you do matters and can change the direction and path of not only the people you encounter, but also the people they encounter, and on it goes.

Choose your words and deeds wisely!

Do a random act of kindness for someone each day. Fill in the blank with what you did.

Day 1 – Today I _____

_____

Day 2 – Today I _____

_____

Day 3 – Today I _____

_____

Day 4 – Today I _____

_____

Day 5 – Today I _____

_____

Day 6 – Today I _____

_____

Day 7 – Today I _____

_____

How did you feel about yourself as you did random acts of kindness? Do you think it made a difference to the receivers? If so, how?

_____

_____

_____

_____

_____

_____

Spend Some Time in Nature

Being in nature among trees, plants, and water can have a calming effect on your body and nervous system. A study published in the *Proceedings of the National Academy of Science* found that people who walked for 90 minutes in a natural area, as opposed to participants who walked in a high-traffic urban setting, showed decreased activity in a region of the brain associated with a key factor in depression.

Enjoy the beauty of nature. Regardless of the weather, bundle up if it is cold and feel the cool air on your cheeks; and if the sun is out, feel the warmth of it on your face. Is there a place you can go, a park, the mountains, or the beach? Somewhere where you can connect with nature, take in its beauty, and listen to the sounds of birds, the wind, the waves, or the quiet?

Here are some ways to spend in nature:

- Go for a walk or run

- Go for a hike

- Go for a bike ride

- Go skiing

- Meditate outside

- Eat outside

- Camp overnight

Spend some time in nature this week and notice how you feel. Then write your feeling word to complete the sentence for each day, "I spent time in nature and felt _____."

Day 1 – I spent time in nature and felt _____

Day 2 – I spent time in nature and felt _____

Day 3 – I spent time in nature and felt _____

Day 4 – I spent time in nature and felt _____

Day 5 – I spent time in nature and felt _____

Day 6 – I spent time in nature and felt _____

Day 7 – I spent time in nature and felt _____

What happens when you spend some time out in nature? What impact does it have on your thoughts, mood, and feelings?

Get It Done Now - It's Good for Your Health!

Are you a "get it done now or get it done later" person? Did you know that it takes more energy not to do something than just to do it, especially if you are going to do it anyway?

Do you ever think about the amount of energy you use not to do something you need to do? Some people may call this procrastination or laziness. It doesn't matter what you label it. Putting off doing what you need to do can negatively affect your health and well-being.

When you put off doing what needs to get done by avoiding it, or doing other non-important things, internally, you may be building increased levels of stress, worry, anger, resentment, and fear that you won't get it done or feelings of inadequacy.

What would it be like if you just did the task? Or, what if you stopped all the ways you keep "busy" doing other things to avoid feeling your feelings while neglecting what you need to do?

Try it today. Do something you've been putting off NOW!

Fill in the blank with what you do each day. Have it be something you've been putting off, avoiding, or stressing over. Something that you're going to do anyway, and it would be better for you if you did it sooner rather than putting it off until later.

Day 1 – Today I _____

Day 2 – Today I _____

Day 3 – Today I _____

Day 4 – Today I _____

Day 5 – Today I _____

Day 6 – Today I _____

Day 7 – Today I _____

What was the impact of taking action sooner rather than later? How did it feel to push through your resistance? What were the benefits to you? Did you feel less stressed or have more time for other things?

_____

_____

_____

Childhood Experiences Shape Who We Become

Forgotten childhood joy robs us of positive memories that can spark a renewed interest as an adult, bringing joy back into your life. Did you know that adults, when seeking career counseling, are usually asked about childhood interests? Following your interests and passions can lead to a satisfying career or hobby.

What were you interested in as a child?

If you have a hard time coming up with what you loved as a child, here are some "memory joggers" for adults to explore and foster their interests and passions:

Enjoying the outdoors – spend time in nature by going outside in your backyard, visit a park, the mountains, desert, or beach. Run through the grass, collect rocks or shells, or pick up trash. Go camping, make mud pies, build a sand or dirt castle, dig a big hole and fill it with water then put your feet in it, or build roads in the dirt for toy trucks and cars.

Sports – try a new sport: badminton, ping-pong, tennis, golf, baseball, basketball, or volleyball. Or join an adult sports team. See local professional or college teams play live games. Make your own fun Olympics with activities like jumping rope, hula-hooping, doing jumping jacks, hopping on one foot, or relay races. You could also read books about your favorite sports teams, players, athletes, or coaches.

Animals – visit a zoo, volunteer at an animal rescue organization, foster a dog or cat, offer to walk a neighbor's dog, take horseback riding lessons.

Gardening – grow a garden of vegetables, herbs, or flowers. Participate in or start a community garden. Ask a neighbor with a garden if you could help maintain it.

Cooking – find some new recipes to cook, create your own recipe, take a cooking class, make a cookbook with your favorite recipes.

Reading – find a good book to read, a mystery, drama, or biography, visit your local library, start a book club, browse a used book store.

Writing – write poetry, a short story, a children's book, a blog, or keep a journal.

Photography – take pictures, frame some, make a collage, choose a theme to photograph, take black and white photos, edit photos on the computer.

Playing games – play board games, cards, or make your own themed game with cardboard and dice.

Puzzles – do a jigsaw puzzle, word search, sudoku, or other word- or number-related puzzles.

Music – listen to different types of music, see a live concert or performance, watch musical movies, take singing lessons, learn to play the piano or another instrument, read biographies about musicians.

Dance – put on some music and dance, take lessons, go out dancing, watch dance shows on TV, or see a live dance performance.

Acting – play charades, write a skit and perform it, or make a short video using your smartphone to record it.

Swimming/water play – create your own Olympics with a friendly neighborhood swim contest, have a parent/kid race, or join an adult swim team. Play Marco-Polo, pool volleyball, toss a beach ball, get out the water guns, run through the sprinklers, or play catch with water balloons.

Computers – learn how they work, or learn a new computer program, take a class, create a website.

Science – get several books about science from the library and find some science experiments to do at home, visit a science museum, take a class about an area of science that interests you.

What did you love as a child? Spend some time reflecting on your childhood interests and passions, and then do what you are inspired to do!

This week, identify one area of interest and write it below. Then each day fill in the blank with something specific you do from that area of interest or the step you take to get involved in that area of interest. This can be done by researching what's available, gathering information and knowledge, and planning how to get involved.

My area of interest is:

_____

Day 1 – Today I _____

Day 2 – Today I _____

Day 3 – Today I _____

Day 4 – Today I _____

Day 5 – Today I _____

Day 6 – Today I _____

Day 7 – Today I _____

How was it to commit to your area of interest? What did you discover about yourself and next steps? What are your next steps?

_____
_____

How Overwhelm Led to a Self-Discovery

I needed a new lamp for my office and found myself overwhelmed by all the choices. I started to question whether it was just about the fact that there were too many choices or if there was something else going on. I approached my lamp search like I do most things for me, find something practical that will do the job and not cost too much money.

While I could adapt to any lamp, I didn't want to on this purchase. I didn't want to settle for a lamp I wouldn't like as much as the one I had. This was so much bigger than just a lamp purchase. It was me deciding to shift the familiar pattern of adapting to something that wasn't what I wanted or settling for something I didn't truly like.

I realized that what was missing in my lamp search was ME. Then I wondered what it would be like if I started my search for a lamp by looking for something that was appealing to me, and that I would want to look at daily. I eventually found the right lamp for me, and I like it even better than my previous one!

It felt so good to make this shift from being practical and settling for good enough, to having my lamp search be about what I would enjoy!

Think about how you approach buying things for yourself. Ask yourself if you are making a purchase from a place of or practicality or lack and scarcity rather than searching for something you truly desire and will enjoy.

This week, notice your buying decisions and how you decide what to purchase. Put a check mark next to each day that you take the time to become aware of your reasons for buying something.

_____ Day 1   _____ Day 4   _____ Day 7

_____ Day 2   _____ Day 5

_____ Day 3   _____ Day 6

What did you learn about yourself around buying? Do you use this same pattern of thinking in other areas of your life? What will you do differently, if anything, now that you are aware of your buying pattern?

_____

_____

_____

_____

_____

_____

_____

_____

_____

_____

_____

_____

_____

_____

_____

_____

_____

_____

_____

_____

_____

_____

_____

_____

_____

_____

_____

_____

_____

_____

_____

_____

_____

_____

_____

_____

_____

_____

_____

_____

_____

_____

_____

_____

_____

_____

_____

_____

_____

_____

_____

_____

_____

_____

_____

You Live How You Breathe

I was once told, "You live how you breathe." At that time, I was barely breathing enough to stay alive. I wasn't sick or struck with an illness, yet I could go for hours without taking a full breath. I probably developed this breathing pattern in my early childhood as a way of coping, which explains why I've had a hard time feeling my feelings. Shallow breathing kept me from feeling sadness, fear, anxiety, and grief. It also prevented me from feeling happiness, joy, contentment, and a connection with myself and others. When I began to pay more attention to my breath, I felt more relaxed and peaceful.

Like me, many other people restrict their breath and could benefit from deeper breathing. Deep breathing, according to some researchers, is an effective, drug-free way of reducing stress and feelings of anxiety. The following is a breathing exercise from the American Academy of Family Physicians:

1. Lie down flat on your back, placing one hand on your stomach and one hand on your chest.

2. Slowly breathe in, making sure your stomach rises, but your chest remains flat.

3. Hold your breath for a second or two.

4. Slowly exhale and allow your stomach to drop.

5. Repeat for three to five breaths.

Breathing into your tummy puts you back in touch with yourself and your full range of feelings! I encourage you to allow yourself to breathe, breathe, breathe!

This week, put a check mark next to each day that you take time to breathe deeply.

_____ Day 1   _____ Day 4   _____ Day 7

_____ Day 2   _____ Day 5

_____ Day 3   _____ Day 6

What did you notice by breathing deeply? What feelings were you in touch with? How did your body feel? What could you do to make a commitment to become aware of your breathing going forward?

_____

_____

_____

_____

_____

_____

_____

_____

_____

_____

_____

_____

_____

_____

_____

_____

_____

_____

_____

_____

_____

_____

_____

_____

_____

_____

_____

_____

_____

_____

Stargazing, Sunrises, and Sunsets

When was the last time you looked at the night sky, I mean really took the time to notice the stars and the moon? Or marveled at a beautiful sunrise or sunset? Stargazing and watching a sunrise or sunset are activities that can put you in touch with your sense of wonder.

While I was on an African safari, we went on a night tour to see the nocturnal animals. While the animals were great to see, words could not describe how I felt seeing the night sky. There were so many stars that it didn't seem real. It was spectacular and something I will remember for the rest of my life!

If you're an early riser, take a moment to notice the sunrise, and in the evening, catch the sunset. Admire the colors, as if the sky was painted. If you're awake at night, check out the stars and the moon.

There is something magical about looking at the sky by day or by night. Watching the sun rise or set can stir up a feeling of awe.

Take some time this week to notice the sky!

Put a check mark next to each day this week that you take the time to notice a sunrise, sunset, or the stars at night.

_____ Day 1   _____ Day 4   _____ Day 7

_____ Day 2   _____ Day 5

_____ Day 3   _____ Day 6

What was it like to notice the sky? How did you feel? What thoughts did you have?

_____

_____

_____

_____

_____

_____

_____

_____

_____

_____

_____

_____

_____

_____

_____

_____

_____

_____

_____

_____

_____

_____

_____

_____

_____

_____

_____

_____

_____

_____

_____

_____

_____

_____

_____

_____

_____

_____

_____

_____

_____

The Brain Doesn't Know the Difference

The brain doesn't know the difference between if you actually did something or just thought about it. Research has shown that without a stressful event actually happening, you can create anxiety along with the chemical release of the stress hormones cortisol and adrenaline, just by thinking about such an event.

The converse is true. When you have pleasant, calm, or happy thoughts, the biochemical production and release of serotonin and dopamine occur. How you think has a direct correlation to how you feel. Since your thoughts create a cascade of chemical releases, and you know your thoughts can produce healthy or unhealthy hormones, you truly do have some control over your well-being.

Here are some ways to shift to calmer, happier thinking:

- Focus on gratitude

- Be thankful

- Look for your happiest moment of the day

- Meditate

- Ease up on perfectionism

- Laugh and play more

Remind yourself throughout the day to check in with your thoughts. You could do this whenever you reach for the phone to make a call, stop at a red light, before you eat, or when you wake up or go to sleep.

If you are feeling stressed, it may be time to look more closely at your thinking and choose to look at situations in a more positive light. Remember, it's good for your health!

This week put a check mark next to each day that you turn a stressful thought to a more positive one or use one of the ways listed to shift to calmer, happier thinking.

_____ Day 1   _____ Day 4   _____ Day 7

_____ Day 2   _____ Day 5

_____ Day 3   _____ Day 6

What changed as you used the suggestions to shift stressful thoughts? What was most effective to shift your thoughts? What can you commit to using on an ongoing basis?

What Have You Done for Fun Lately?

What brings out the fun in you? Do you allow yourself to enjoy activities without being concerned about results? Are playing games fun? What about doing puzzles? Do you like social fun?

When was the last time you got so involved in an activity that you lost all track of time? This is called being in flow. Proposed by Mihály Csíkszentmihályi, the Positive Psychology concept of flow is the "mental state of operation in which a person in an activity is fully immersed in a feeling of energized focus, full involvement, and success in the process of the activity." The state of flow can happen while creating something artistic, writing, cooking, building something, playing a sport, walking or running, playing a game, gardening, or doing almost any activity alone or with others.

There's plenty to be serious about in the adult world. The problems of the world may not be solved by worrying about them. They just may be resolved by us connecting with ourselves, having more fun, and getting along better with one another!

Put a check mark next to each day that you do something fun. How can you make something you're already doing fun, like cooking, driving somewhere, or going for a walk?

_____ Day 1   _____ Day 4   _____ Day 7

_____ Day 2   _____ Day 5

_____ Day 3   _____ Day 6

What did you do for fun this week? What was the impact of focusing on making something fun? What other ideas do you have about incorporating more fun into your life?

_____

_____

_____

_____

_____

_____

_____

_____

_____

_____

_____

_____

_____

_____

What Shall I Do with It?

Have you ever had something that you valued so much that you wanted to do something special with it, and by the time you decided, the opportunity passed? The fruit aged, the flower you were going to cut and put in a vase wilted in the heat, or the shoes or outfit you were saving for a special occasion were never worn.

There are many reasons why you might have difficulty deciding on how to enjoy something special:

- When it's gone, you won't have it anymore

- It's too special to use or wear

- It was expensive

- It's one of a kind and irreplaceable

- Fear of ruining it, wearing it out, or using it up

Enjoy something special today, use it, look at it, or wear it. What are you waiting for?

Make each day this week a "special day" by using something you've been waiting to use. Wear the clothes or shoes, use the good dishes and glasses, etc. Fill in the blank next to each day with what you do or use that makes it special.

Day 1 – Today I _____

Day 2 – Today I _____

Day 3 – Today I _____

Day 4 – Today I _____

Day 5 – Today I _____

Day 6 – Today I _____

Day 7 – Today I _____

What was it like for you to use the "good stuff?" How did that change your relationship to the things that you value?

_____

_____

_____

_____

_____

_____

_____

_____

_____

_____

_____

_____

_____

_____

_____

_____

_____

_____

_____

_____

_____

_____

_____

_____

_____

_____

_____

_____

What Would You Be?

Here's a fun way for family members or friends to support each other in "trying on" *being* a different way in one area of your life for the next seven days. Select one of the following or come up with your own:

Be abundance – spend some time each day visualizing abundance in your all areas of your life: personally, professionally, financially, physically, socially and spiritually. Anchor in the feeling of having plenty of what it is you desire, including the abundance of time.

Be peace – do things that create inner peace. Meditate daily, do breathing exercises, take a warm bath by candlelight, listen to calming music, do yoga.

Be happy – focus on being happy and cultivating happiness by keeping a happiness journal where you write three to five happy moments from your day or share your happiest moments of the day with a friend. Each day look for things that make you smile!

Be a healthy eater – select some healthy recipes to prepare and eat throughout the week. Choose to eat a serving of fruit each day, eat whole grains, try a new vegetable, or eat a salad.

Be an athlete – do some form of physical activity each day. It can be the same thing every day or something different. You might challenge yourself to improve over the week by seeing if you can increase the number of steps you take daily using a pedometer, or the amount of time or distance you walk or run. Or get a friend or two together and shoot hoops, play tennis, kick a soccer ball, or play catch.

Be giving – do something for others each day. It could be as simple as writing a note of appreciation, picking a flower to give someone, making a fruit basket for a friend, or volunteering.

Be beauty – each day do something to for your appearance. Your smile (brush and floss your teeth daily), your hair (deep condition and style it), your face (give yourself a facial or at least wash and moisturize your face daily), your skin (put lotion on your arms and legs), your feet (soak your feet, then rub lotion on them).

Keep it fun, positive, and supportive!

What will you be this week? Choose one of the above that feels the most relevant to you to "try on" this week and write it in the space below. (You can always come back to this exercise and choose a different way of being for a different week.) Then, each day, fill in the blank with what you did "to be" what you have chosen. You can do the same activity each day or mix it up, as long as you keep the same theme.

This week I choose to be:

_____

Day 1 – Today I _____

Day 2 – Today I _____

Day 3 – Today I _____

Day 4 – Today I _____

Day 5 – Today I _____

Day 6 – Today I _____

Day 7 – Today I _____

What was it like for you to be what you chose? What is the most important thing you learned from this experience? What did you learn that could be the start of a new beginning?

_____

_____

_____

_____

_____

_____

Clue, Sorry, Scrabble

When was the last time you played an old-fashioned board game? Playing board games can be a great way to bond with your children, grandchildren, adult children, or other adults. Many games such as Clue, Scrabble, and Monopoly have a junior version for younger children.

Here are some suggestions for enjoyable playing:

1. Keep it fun.

2. Team up if you have too many people or pair a child with a teen or adult for more advanced games.

3. Don't worry about the outcome and who is going to win. Just like an athlete, play your game, do your best, and don't cave in to pressure. Stay focused on the game and your turn rather than on winning.

What if the winner was the person or team that had the most fun, win or lose? Play for the pure enjoyment and entertainment that games are designed for.

Make plans with someone you want to play a game with. Calendar it, get out the game and have fun playing. Fill in the blank next to each day with the game you played or if you didn't play a game, write the plans you made with someone to play a game.

Day 1 – Today I _____

Day 2 – Today I _____

Day 3 – Today I _____

Day 4 – Today I _____

Day 5 – Today I _____

Day 6 – Today I _____

Day 7 – Today I _____

Did you have fun? What made it fun? What could you have done to make it more fun? Have playing games improved your relationships? How so?

What Are You Looking Forward To?

No matter what your age, having something to look forward to that's fun, special, or different can help you get through your day-to-day routine. Anticipating an upcoming event, outing, or get-together builds excitement and may even cause you to daydream, similar to being in meditation.

When you have something to look forward to, you may experience yourself smiling more, being kinder to others and yourself, and more tolerant of what would generally annoy you. In other words, having something to look forward to may have a positive effect on your happiness, well-being, and even your productivity.

Calendar things to look forward to today, tomorrow, next week, next month, and next year.

Here's a list of possible activities to get you started:

- Meet a friend for coffee, tea, or a walk

- Downtime to use as you choose

- A morning or afternoon of golf, hiking, or biking

- A day at a museum, an amusement park, or the zoo

- Bowling, skating, or playing miniature golf

- Host a game night and invite some friends over to play

- A vacation to another area, state, or country

- How you will celebrate your birthday

- Attend a live event such as a concert, play, or sporting event

- A drive to the mountains or beach

- Being pampered with a massage, facial, manicure or pedicure

- A pot-luck dinner with a few friends

- An overnight weekend get-away

- Try a new restaurant

- Train for and participate in a 5k, 10k, half marathon, or full marathon

- Celebrate the next holiday on the calendar

- Play tourist in your town or a nearby city

What are you looking forward to? May you, your friends, and family, have many wonderful things to look forward to!

Make a list of several things you'd like to do over the next days, weeks, and months. Then get out your calendar and schedule them. Fill in the blank with what you did next to each day that you take steps to have things to look forward to.

Day 1 – Today I _____

Day 2 – Today I _____

Day 3 – Today I _____

Day 4 – Today I _____

Day 5 – Today I _____

Day 6 – Today I _____

Day 7 – Today I _____

By having something to look forward to, how did this exercise shift your mindset? What type of things are you most looking forward to?

Whose Problem Is It?

If you are like me, you may find yourself sometimes taking on what's not yours. If you like solving problems, think you have a lot to offer, and enjoy helping others, you might be doing someone a disservice. This happens when the problem isn't yours to solve, and when others can do for themselves.

Here's an actual description of the effects of a mother doing too much for her daughter.

I had an adult client in her 40s who had difficulties making decisions, even basic decisions. She had made a series of poor choices and came to me for help. It didn't take long for me to assess the root of her problem. When she was growing up her mother knew best, and rather than giving her choices or opportunities to make her own decisions; her mother made them for her.

The result of not learning to make decisions in childhood left this woman unable to trust herself, always second guessing her decisions, and feeling bad when things didn't work out. In our work together she was able to learn how to tune into herself for guidance and let go of the need to have someone else make decisions for her. For the first time in her life, she felt capable of solving problems on her own.

When you solve someone else's problems:

1. You take away the opportunity for them to solve their own problems and build confidence, skills, and resiliency.

2. You prevent them from struggling to grow their wings and find their way.

3. You may be giving the message that they aren't capable or that you don't trust them to solve their problems.

4. You may be focusing on them to avoid dealing with your own problems. To find out, ask yourself, "Whose life am I living?"

Just think how life would be if everyone took care of what was theirs to handle. It would free up people who tend to over-do and allow others the chance to learn and grow.

It may be hard to let go of this pattern. This week, become aware of what you do for others and your motivations behind your actions. Each day ask yourself, "Am I solving a problem that's not mine?" Then put a check mark next to each day that you thought about the way you help others.

_____ Day 1 – "Am I solving a problem that's not mine?"

_____ Day 2 – "Am I solving a problem that's not mine?"

_____ Day 3 – "Am I solving a problem that's not mine?"

_____ Day 4 – "Am I solving a problem that's not mine?"

_____ Day 5 – "Am I solving a problem that's not mine?"

_____ Day 6 – "Am I solving a problem that's not mine?"

_____ Day 7 – "Am I solving a problem that's not mine?"

What did you learn about yourself by asking, "Am I solving a problem that's not mine?" Did you make any changes during the week as a result? If so, what caused you to modify your behavior and what changes did you make?

_____

_____

_____

_____

_____

_____

_____

_____

_____

_____

Put Your Oxygen Mask On

Creating a healthy lifestyle is like putting on your oxygen mask. When you take care of your basic needs you have so much more to give, making you a better partner, parent, friend, employee or employer, and just a better human being.

Let's start with breathing. Deep breathing calms your nervous system, reduces stress, and restores clearer thinking. Meditation and breathing exercises that include slow, deep breathing are like putting on an oxygen mask. Next to breathing, eating well and often enough are vital for your body. When you get too busy, it's easy to choose something quick to eat that may not be very good for the functioning of your body. Aim for more vegetables, fruit, and whole grains, and remember to hydrate with plenty of water. For snacks, apples, pears, and almonds are quick and easy to eat at home, when traveling, at work, or when out and about.

Sleep is also vital. In fact, it may be one of the most important things you could do for your body. Getting adequate sleep allows for regeneration, repair, and healing of your cells. Sleep also affects your hormones, which regulate your body's systems and everything from mood to weight. Without your oxygen mask on you can't respond to an emergency, let alone daily life. Don't you want to be your best? It's so simple – eat, sleep, breathe!

This week, focus on one or two ways to take better care of you. Write what you did in the spaces that follow after you eat better, sleep more, or breathe deeply.

Day 1 – Today I _____

Day 2 – Today I _____

Day 3 – Today I _____

Day 4 – Today I _____

Day 5 – Today I _____

Day 6 – Today I _____

Day 7 – Today I _____

What did you notice about how you felt physically? What did you notice about how you felt mentally? What do you want to do more of, ongoing? What are you willing to commit to?

_____

_____

_____

_____

Why Rate Your Anger?

In Week 22, "What's Under All That Anger?" you learned about how anger is a secondary emotion, and under anger is the primary emotion, fear, hurt, or sadness. Anger is a great emotion to explore. It can give you information about how you feel about something and the energy to do something about it. It can also get in the way of clear thinking and decision making. For people who feel fear, hurt, and sadness, but don't feel anger, you could ask yourself, "If I was angry about something, what might that be?"

When was the last time you felt steaming mad and ready to blow? On a scale of 1-10, low levels of anger and frustration are a 1-4, while higher levels of anger, above a seven, can feel intense, and may impair your judgment and decision-making abilities. When you are aware of how you feel, and to what degree you feel angry, then you can know how best to act rather than to react.

With low to mid-range levels of anger, it may be enough to look at a situation and consider your options. One option may be to accept what is, rather than how you want it to be or wish it was. For example, if you have a challenging child, it would be wise to accept and parent "that child," rather than the one you wish you had. The same concept can be applied to relationships with a mate, friends, and people you work with, as well as with other life situations.

If your level of anger is a seven or above, it's wise to hold off making important decisions or driving until you feel calmer. Take a time-out (See Have You Ever Put Yourself in a Time-out? – Week 19, on page 75) from the situation and do something physical, go for a walk, a run, do jumping jacks, or climb a flight of stairs. If you need immediate relief, try washing your hands in ice-cold water. It can often shift the way you feel.

Notice and rate your anger each day this week on a scale of 1-10. Then circle the primary emotion you are feeling (fear, hurt, or sadness). Lastly, write what you did to reduce your anger. You might choose to pause and take a time-out to regroup your thoughts and feelings before taking action, do something physical, wash your hands in ice-cold water, or decide to accept your situation and let go of the anger.

Day 1 – My level of anger today is _____. What's under the anger is: (circle one) fear, hurt, or sadness. I reduced my anger by

_____

Day 2 – My level of anger today is _____. What's under the anger is: (circle one) fear, hurt, or sadness. I reduced my anger by

_____

Day 3 – My level of anger today is _____. What's under the anger is: (circle one) fear, hurt, or sadness. I reduced my anger by

_____

Day 4 – My level of anger today is _____. What's under the anger is: (circle one) fear, hurt, or sadness. I reduced my anger by

_____

Day 5 – My level of anger today is _____. What's under the anger is: (circle one) fear, hurt, or sadness. I reduced my anger by

_____

Day 6 – My level of anger today is _____. What's under the anger is: (circle one) fear, hurt, or sadness. I reduced my anger by

_____

Day 7 – My level of anger today is _____. What's under the anger is: (circle one) fear, hurt, or sadness. I reduced my anger by

_____

What did you discover about yourself and anger? How did this week shift your pattern with anger?

_____

_____

_____

_____

Sticker Charts for Adults

Sticker charts have been used for everything from potty training to doing chores. Perhaps you used them as a child or with your children to focus on homework, bathing, or good behavior. They can aid in creating new routines until they become a habit.

Adults can use a "check-off chart" to develop healthy habits. It could include any healthy habit you want to focus on such as exercise, reading for pleasure, daily meditation, journal writing, or going to bed by a particular time.

Have fun with your own "check-off chart." It's not about perfection. Use your chart to remind yourself to engage in habits that nourish you. Not every activity needs to be done daily. You may choose to do something only three or four days a week.

Praise yourself for your efforts during the week, and remember to reward yourself, too!

> # Download your own
> ## "Weekly Check-off Chart" at
> ## www.phyllisginsberg.com/resources

Choose one or two healthy habits to focus on. Write them on your "Weekly Check-off Chart." Put a check mark next to each day that you use your check-off chart as a reminder.

_____ Day 1 – Today I used my check-off chart.

_____ Day 2 – Today I used my check-off chart.

_____ Day 3 – Today I used my check-off chart.

_____ Day 4 – Today I used my check-off chart.

_____ Day 5 – Today I used my check-off chart.

_____ Day 6 – Today I used my check-off chart.

_____ Day 7 – Today I used my check-off chart.

What did you track on your check-off chart and why was it important to you? What was the impact of using your check-off chart?

_____

_____

_____

_____

_____

_____

_____

_____

_____

_____

_____

_____

_____

_____

_____

_____

_____

_____

_____

_____

_____

_____

_____

_____

_____

_____

_____

Perfectly Imperfect

When I was 7 years old, I spent an hour cleaning our broiler pan because I wanted to. It had been so dirty, and I was able to get it to sparkle and shine like new! I got lots of praise for my accomplishment, and it was a defining moment that anchored in my belief that doing things perfectly, especially cleaning, is how I get positive attention and feel loved in my family.

I used to believe that I had to be perfect in everything I did and in how I appeared. It wasn't okay to make a mistake or to not do a thorough job. That's what I was taught, and it was reinforced with high expectations and punishments.

Perfectionism is a trait learned in childhood and carried into adulthood. Unfortunately, striving to do things perfectly often takes more time and energy than if you allowed yourself to do a "good enough" job. Perfectionism can put you in a chronic state of feeling stressed and anxious from the pressure you put on yourself or the pressure you perceive others put on you.

Do you hold yourself back from inviting people over because your home isn't straightened up or spotless with everything in its place? Or have you refused to participate in an activity that looks like fun because you aren't very good at it? What are you telling yourself will happen if you don't live up to that perfection?

A good question to ask yourself is, "Regarding my perfectionism, who might I be trying to impress, or has it simply become a habit or way of life?" We tend to do what was done to us because that was our childhood programming. Now that you are more aware, you can look at your patterns and decide to change them, if you choose.

Perfectionists miss out on enjoying the process along the way and seeing the beauty in things rather than the flaws. There is a better way. It's okay to be good enough, for your living space to be clean enough. It can be important to slow down and not spend so much time on a task to make it so perfect that you end up resenting the amount of time spent on it.

If you wait for everything to be perfect, you will miss out on the enjoyment of life. Set your priorities and determine where good enough will suffice. And while you are at it, perhaps you can allow others to be a little less than perfect too!

Become aware this week of where you have perfectionistic traits. Then see if you can ease up, just a little bit, and allow yourself to enjoy "good enough." Fill in the blank with what you do next to each day that you think about and ease up on perfectionism.

Day 1 – Today I _____

Day 2 – Today I _____

Day 3 – Today I _____

Day 4 – Today I _____

Day 5 – Today I _____

Day 6 – Today I _____

Day 7 – Today I _____

What did you learn about perfectionism for yourself? What shifted in your mindset? What do you envision doing differently so you can experience more enjoyment in your life?

_____

_____

_____

_____

_____

_____

_____

_____

_____

_____

How Do You Define Yourself?

Do you ever stop to consider how you think about the events of your day? The things that go well and fall into place AND the things that go wrong and challenge you? What do you focus on? Do you define yourself by your mistakes or your achievements, the things that go wrong or the things that go right?

It's so easy to get caught up in the negative things that happen. Just getting out of your home in the morning can be a challenge, then if you get stuck in traffic, are running late, forget something important... The list goes on, and all these mini events add up. If this happens more days than not, and you find yourself focusing on all the things that go wrong, there is hope!

Here are some suggestions you can try:

1. Turn your focus to the things that go right, just like you would turn your radio to different stations; from rap to jazz or country to classical. Look and listen for the positive things that occur

throughout your day, and just as you would have noticed the things that went wrong, see if you can tune into the things that go right.

2. You may also want to look at what you have control over and what you don't. Can you change your routine? Can you plan to be better prepared for your day? Can you delegate a task to someone else at home or work? Can you handle a difficult person in a new way? Might it feel better to slow down rather than rush around or multitask?

3. Look at how other people handle life's challenges, especially people who focus on what is going right. There is a lot that can be learned!

This week, notice where you put your focus – on what goes well or what doesn't, on what you have control over or what you don't. Each day write three things that went well for you.

Day 1

1. _____

2. _____

3. _____

Day 2

1. _____

2. _____

3. _____

Day 3

1. _____

2. _____

3. _____

Day 4

1. _____

2. _____

3. _____

Day 5

1. _____

2. _____

3. _____

Day 6

1. _____

2. _____

3. _____

Day 7

1. _____

2. _____

3. _____

What did you learn about yourself by writing what went well? Did it change where you put your focus? As the week went on was it easier to focus on what goes right? What implications could this activity have on the way you define what happens? Did doing this exercise change the way you think about events and what you have control over? How so?

_____

_____

_____

_____

_____

_____

_____

_____

_____

_____

_____

_____

_____

_____

_____

_____

_____

_____

_____

_____

Rewards for Adults, Children, and Teens

In many cultures, food is used as a reward. It's possible that non-food-related rewards may work better as a natural way of reinforcing positive behavior. Rather than rewarding with food, use words, activities, a book, outings, or athletic apparel and equipment.

The following are ways of rewarding and praising yourself and others:

Reward and praise with words:

- Great job! You're terrific!

- I like the choice you made to _____.

- It was fun to watch your team play so well.

- I like the effort you are making toward your goal.

Reward to promote physical activity with:

- A jump rope, a hula-hoop, a kite, a baseball and glove, a football, a soccer ball, a basketball, a badminton set, a Frisbee, a volleyball, or pool toys

- A yoga mat or small exercise weights

- An athletic shirt, shorts, socks, or shoes

- A book about a sport, a sports team, or individual athlete

Reward with outings:

- To play at the park, hike in the mountains, bike along the beach, wander the zoo, or run around at an amusement park

- To see a live sporting event; a baseball, basketball, football or hockey game

Reward by pampering with:

- A manicure, pedicure, facial, or massage at home, a salon, or a spa

- Time to read a book you've wanted to read or to work on a creative project you enjoy (knitting, sewing, painting, drawing, etc.)

When you use non-food-related rewards, it gives you and others something tangible or an experience that can last much longer than a meal out or an ice cream!

This week, reward yourself and others with words of praise, a new piece of equipment, an outing, or something special. Complete the following sentences each day, filling in who you rewarded (yourself or someone else), with what, and what happened as a result:

Day 1

Today I rewarded _____(who) with
_____(what).
And _____ happened.

Day 2

Today I rewarded _____(who) with
_____(what).
And _____ happened.

Day 3

Today I rewarded _____(who) with
_____(what).
And _____ happened.

Day 4

Today I rewarded _____(who) with
_____(what).
And _____ happened.

Day 5

Today I rewarded _____(who) with
_____(what).
And _____ happened.

Day 6

Today I rewarded _____(who) with
_____(what).
And _____ happened.

Day 7

Today I rewarded _____(who) with
_____(what).
And _____ happened.

How did rewarding yourself and others impact your relationship with
you and them? What type of rewards did you like giving to others
the best, and receiving (from yourself)?

_____

_____

_____

_____

_____

_____

_____

_____

Make-Believe for Adults

Play is an essential part of childhood development and has also been shown to have a positive impact on adults. One form of play is pretending to be someone or something that you are not. Do you remember as a child make-believing you were an animal, a doctor, a mom or dad? And when you got older, taking on the role of a favorite athlete, movie star, television character, or singer?

When you "try on" a new identity, especially of someone who you admire for their positive characteristics, it can build confidence and a positive self-image. It may even help you get through tasks you don't like to do. Imagine being a pirate looking for buried treasure as you clean out a drawer or closet or that you're in a cooking competition as you prepare dinner.

One way to increase the amount of physical activity you get is by pretending you are a top athlete in your favorite sport, scoring, breaking a record, or winning a game. The most important part of playing "make-believe" is having fun, and who knows, you just might find that you actually are talented at what you are pretending to be!

What or who would you like to "make-believe" you are this week?

_____

Each day this week spend some time playing "make-believe," even if it's only for a few minutes. Notice how you feel and what you do.

Day 1

Today while playing make-believe I was (what)_____

and I did _____.

Day 2

Today while playing make-believe I was (what)_____

and I did _____.

Day 3

Today while playing make-believe I was (what)_____

and I did _____.

Day 4

Today while playing make-believe I was (what)_____

and I did _____.

Day 5

Today while playing make-believe I was (what)_____

and I did _____.

Day 6

Today while playing make-believe I was (what)_____

and I did _____.

Day 7

Today while playing make-believe I was (what)_____

and I did _____.

In what ways did playing make-believe change your behavior? How did you feel taking on a new role? More capable? More confident? What was the impact of playing make-believe?

_____

_____

_____

_____

_____

_____

_____

_____

_____

_____

_____

_____

_____

_____

It's All in How You Show Up

Are you the type of person who shows up to a situation ready to interact and initiate conversation or are you more comfortable waiting on the sidelines to see what is going to happen and how events will unfold?

Not everyone is outgoing. You may find yourself more outgoing when you are with people who you are familiar with. If you often feel invisible and are the one who waits for others to approach you and say hello first, there is another way to show up. Just because you have been a certain way doesn't mean you must continue to be that way.

What would it be like to greet your day, greet yourself, and greet others with enthusiasm, wonder, curiosity, and interest? Imagine showing up to meet life and to create your day rather than waiting to see what the day brings.

You might miss out waiting for life to happen. What if the other person is waiting for you too? Be the first to say good morning, hello, or good day. Show up for YOU and watch what YOU make happen!

Put a check mark next to each day that you greet the day, greet yourself, and greet others with enthusiasm, wonder, curiosity, and interest.

_____ Day 1   _____ Day 4   _____ Day 7

_____ Day 2   _____ Day 5

_____ Day 3   _____ Day 6

How did this change your perspective of yourself and your ability to connect with others? What was the most challenging part of "showing up?" How can you make it easier to show up for your life?

_____

_____

_____

_____

_____

_____

_____

_____

_____

_____

_____

_____

_____

Life Lessons from World Series Champs

The San Francisco Giants won the World Series on October 28, 2012, and even if you aren't a baseball fan or into sports you too might be impressed with what I observed. While watching interviews of the MVP of the series, Pablo Sandoval, and other players, I was in awe of how they all seemed to be part of something bigger than themselves, and how they focused on the team effort, not their own.

Imagine how your life would be if the best was brought out in you. If you believed in yourself, to be your authentic self, humbly showcasing your gifts and talents. If you had unwavering faith that you could overcome obstacles, and doubt didn't enter your mind. If you could be yourself, be all that you could be, and have the support of your team.

Life isn't lived in isolation. Like a baseball team, it's not about you. It's about the team, at home, at work, and in your community, with everyone doing their part. Bring your team together and encourage each person to perfect and express their gifts, talents, and skills. Bring out the best in each other. Play hard and have fun. Be gracious when you win. Enjoy the moment, take it in, feel it, and celebrate!

This week spend some time each day imagining what it would be like and feel like to be fully supported by your team while bringing out the best in each other and enjoying the experience. Fill in the blank next to each day with a few words about what you imagined.

Day 1 – Today I imagined _____

Day 2 – Today I imagined _____

Day 3 – Today I imagined _____

Day 4 – Today I imagined _____

Day 5 – Today I imagined _____

Day 6 – Today I imagined _____

Day 7 – Today I imagined _____

What did you learn about yourself when you think about the things you imagined? Did your thoughts change about working as a team at home or at work? How so? What does this tell you about what you want in your relationships? How can you cultivate more of that?

_____

_____

_____

_____

_____

_____

_____

_____

_____

_____

_____

_____

_____

_____

_____

_____

_____

_____

_____

_____

_____

_____

Are You A Rose, Tulip, or Daisy?

Whether you are dating, looking for a new job, seeking a medical practitioner, or cultivating a new friendship, many people overlook the importance of "interviewing each other" to find a good match.

What if we are like flowers; a rose, a tulip, or a daisy, each with our unique qualities, looking for a compatible flower? It doesn't matter if you are a rose, tulip, or daisy. What matters is that you consider who you are, your likes and dislikes, your values and needs, what you are willing to accept and where you aren't willing to compromise.

When you can accept who the other person is, without judgment and without wanting to change them, then you can make a wise decision. Remember, it's about whether you are a good match and what you bring out in each other. Consider the synergy, if you can work together, support each other, and if it indeed is a good fit.

Honor yourself and the other person. Respect your differences if you are not a good match, say so and move on. It may be mutual with no hurt feelings.

Consider who you are at this stage in your life, your likes and dislikes and your needs, wants, and values. Reflect on the people you interact with and if you are a good match. Think about any new people you are seeking. Each day take one step to get more clarity about your needs and the people in your life.

Day 1 – I reflected on _____

Day 2 – I reflected on _____

Day 3 – I reflected on _____

Day 4 – I reflected on _____

Day 5 – I reflected on _____

Day 6 – I reflected on _____

Day 7 – I reflected on _____

What did you learn about yourself? Your likes and dislikes? Your needs and values? Was there a relationship that stood out with too many differences to be compatible? Did thinking about the people in your life reinforce some good matches?

_____

_____

_____

_____

_____

_____

_____

_____

_____

_____

_____

_____

_____

_____

_____

_____

_____

_____

_____

_____

_____

_____

_____

Finding My Way Home

I was leaving San Jose where I had just heard Robert Holden, the author of *Happiness Now*, speak. I was feeling happy, peaceful, and filled with love. I got in my car and expected to be home in just over an hour.

I had confidence in being able to follow the freeway signs and navigate my way home. After 15 minutes I realized I wasn't traveling on the same freeway I took to get there. I followed signs to San Francisco, knowing I was heading in the right direction, yet 30 minutes later I was still second guessing if I was on a route that was going to get me home to the East Bay.

I was frustrated with myself for trusting that I could find my way home. I believed I could do something I'm not a natural at, and I was mad at myself. The wonderful feeling of happiness I had was being taken over by stress and uncertainty. All I wanted was to get back to feeling happy and to get home.

Then, I had an epiphany! I asked myself, "What could I have done different that would have been more loving to myself?" The answer was clear. The most loving thing I could do for myself when unfamiliar with an area would be to take a moment and bring up a map of where I'm going BEFORE driving.

I eventually made it home, as I always do, and I'm looking forward to creating a different experience for myself next time. What's one area of your life where you could be more loving toward yourself?

Each day this week, ask yourself, "What's the most loving thing I could do for myself today?" Then listen for an answer, a thought, or an inspiration. Then do it! Fill in the blank next to each day with what loving act you did for yourself.

Day 1 – The most loving thing I did for myself today was:

_____

Day 2 – The most loving thing I did for myself today was:

_____

Day 3 – The most loving thing I did for myself today was:

_____

Day 4 – The most loving thing I did for myself today was:

_____

Day 5 – The most loving thing I did for myself today was:

_____

Day 6 – The most loving thing I did for myself today was:

_____

Day 7 – The most loving thing I did for myself today was:

_____

What did you learn about yourself? Was there a pattern or theme you discovered? If so, what was it? How did focusing on being loving to yourself each day change your week? How did it change your relationship with yourself and others?

_____

_____

_____

_____

_____

_____

_____

_____

_____

_____

_____

_____

_____

_____

_____

It Could Be As Simple As Changing the Channel

If you don't like something on TV, you change the channel, and if you don't like something in your life, little or big, why not change it, too? If only it could be that simple. Maybe it can be!

Here are some suggestions:

1. Look for a simple solution and if that's not possible consider a variety of options and write them down.

2. Can you easily make the change all at once? Some changes are simple like moving an item that you often use to a more convenient place or adjusting your morning routine or evening routine to include some physical activity, reading, or meditation time.

3. Bigger changes take time to plan, like a job change, a move, significantly improving your health, or changes that impact other people. Create "stepping-stones" to get you to your destination. If you don't feel good about how you have been eating and want to

get healthier, write down the steps necessary to get there. This may include finding healthy recipes, making a menu and a shopping list, buying the items on the list, and preparing the meals.

4. If you don't like something and don't know what to do about it, consider asking someone with experience or expertise for assistance with ideas and options. Remember to also ask friends and family for support.

It may not always be as easy as changing the channel on the TV, but with a little effort, we can improve our lives for the better!

This week, identify one or two things you'd like to change. Look for a simple solution, and if possible, do it. If it's a more significant change, get the information you need to create the stepping-stones to make the change you desire. Fill in the blanks next to each day with the steps you took to shift something specific.

Day 1 – Today I (the step you took) _____

_____ to

improve_____

Day 2 – Today I (the step you took) _____

_____ to

improve_____

Day 3 – Today I (the step you took) _____

_____ to

improve_____

Day 4 – Today I (the step you took) _____

_____ to

improve_____

Day 5 – Today I (the step you took) _____

_____ to

improve_____

Day 6 – Today I (the step you took) _____

_____ to

improve_____

Day 7 – Today I (the step you took) _____

_____ to

improve_____

How do you feel about the changes you made this week or the steps you've taken to make a change? What does that do for your motivation? What will you commit to doing to see the change through?

_____

_____

_____

_____

_____

_____

_____

You Never Really Know If Something Is Good or Bad

A friend of mine fell and injured her arm and knee while preparing to move. Most people would say this was a bad or negative experience. I reached out to my friend, and she gladly accepted my help.

The two days we spent together were a blessing that probably would not have happened had she not gotten injured. We were able to spend time together sorting, packing, and trashing. She got to show me some of her most meaningful artwork and photos, and I came away with some treasures, including two handmade items. On top of that, together we got everything ready for the move ahead of schedule.

This week, when something happens that seems bad or negative, consider that something good may come out of it.

Reflect on past situations in your life that appeared to be bad or negative. See if you can find something good that came from

202 • PHYLLIS GINSBERG

what happened that wouldn't have come about had the "bad" or "negative" event not occurred. Fill in the blanks next to each day with what you thought about and the good things that came from so-called "bad" situations.

Day 1 – The situation I thought about was _____

_____

and what I recognized that was good about it was _____

_____

Day 2 – The situation I thought about was _____

_____

and what I recognized that was good about it was _____

_____

Day 3 – The situation I thought about was _____

_____

and what I recognized that was good about it was _____

_____

Day 4 – The situation I thought about was _____

_____

and what I recognized that was good about it was _____

_____

Day 5 – The situation I thought about was _____

_____

and what I recognized that was good about it was _____

_____

Day 6 – The situation I thought about was _____

_____

and what I recognized that was good about it was _____

_____

Day 7 – The situation I thought about was _____

_____

and what I recognized that was good about it was _____

_____

How did this exercise shift how you look at or approach negative experiences?

_____

_____

_____

_____

_____

_____

_____

_____

_____

_____

Just Ask!

How often do you complain, blame, or criticize when it would be so much easier to just ask for what you want? Why is it so difficult to be direct rather than beating around the bush or expect that people should know what you want? It's no better waiting and focusing on what you don't have while suffering in silence, as this tends to build anger and resentment.

What would it be like to simply ask for what you want? That would require taking responsibility to get your own needs met and being open to the possibility that if you ask, you may not get what you want. Which is worse, feeling the rejection of asking and not getting, or not asking in the first place?

A friend of mine took a class a couple of years ago to learn to be more at ease in social situations, and this was a story she shared with me about asking that changed her beliefs.

I took this class in San Francisco to become more comfortable at networking events. The class homework started with small engagement exercises to perform between classes, and the exercises kept getting more challenging as the weeks went by.

Weeks into the class, I found myself daunted and resistant to doing the homework for the week. We were supposed to approach a completely unknown person and ask them, "what are the first three things you thought of when you saw me?" I was terrified of this exercise because I believed I was imposing on people, but I scraped up my courage and did it anyway. What really surprised me was how happy people were to oblige me, a complete stranger with some really interesting and amazing answers. This was an eye-opener for me. I realized I was capable of asking for things, even of people I didn't know well, and I realized people are often just happy to engage with me and recognized things about me almost instantly. I stopped being afraid to engage strangers too. I highly recommend this exercise to anyone who wants to overcome or is afraid to ask.

No one person can meet all your needs, so it's wise to rely on a variety of people for support. Start by asking people you feel most comfortable with and then move on to others.

This week, practice asking directly for what you want, then fill in the blanks each day with what you asked for and what happened.

Day 1 – Today I asked for _____

and _____

Day 2 – Today I asked for _____

and _____

Day 3 – Today I asked for _____

and _____

Day 4 – Today I asked for _____

and _____

Day 5 – Today I asked for _____

and _____

Day 6 – Today I asked for _____

and _____

Day 7 – Today I asked for _____

and _____

What did you learn about asking for what you want? What could you do to make getting your needs met easier?

_____

_____

_____

_____

_____

_____

_____

_____

_____

I'm All Ears!

When was the last time you felt someone give you their undivided attention? Lives today are so busy, filled with things to do and places to be, electronic devices, and responsibilities, that people rarely stop long enough to acknowledge each other, let alone take the time to listen.

Here are some suggestions to increase connections and improve the quality of your life and theirs:

- Schedule some one-on-one time to talk, laugh, play, and have fun. Or, be spontaneous with who you are with and decide to be all ears!

- Stop what you are doing long enough to be present.

- Make eye contact.

- Give your full attention to the other person so that they may feel seen, heard, and understood.

- Listen with interest.

- Be curious and ask questions.

- Put judgment aside.

- Reply with kindness, encouragement, or something positive.

This week, practice listening with interest and curiosity. Give someone your full attention. To show you listened, ask questions and reply with thoughtfulness. Then fill in the blanks each day with the name of who you listened to and how it was for you.

Day 1 - Today I listened to (who) _____

and I felt _____

Day 2 - Today I listened to (who) _____

and I felt _____

Day 3 - Today I listened to (who) _____

and I felt _____

Day 4 - Today I listened to (who) _____

and I felt _____

Day 5 - Today I listened to (who) _____

and I felt _____

Day 6 - Today I listened to (who) _____

and I felt _____

Day 7 - Today I listened to (who) _____
and I felt _____

How do you feel about your ability to connect with others? Did giving someone your undivided attention improve the conversation? How did this shift your relationship? What else did you notice?

_____
_____
_____
_____
_____
_____
_____
_____
_____
_____
_____
_____
_____
_____
_____
_____
_____
_____
_____
_____

Reflections of the Year

You made it! We're at the end of the weekly readings to makeover your brain, and it's time to see how your Brain Makeover went before moving on to the last week, Brain Compatible New Year's Resolutions – Week 52.

This week is about measuring your progress by taking the **Brain Makeover Follow-Up Assessment,** similar to the one you took at the beginning of the book, and then writing about your reflections of what you learned. This will do two things. First, it will give you feedback to see how far you have come, and second, as you reflect on your progress, it will reinforce, in your brain, the different ways you now think and feel because of the work you have done.

Before you take the follow-up assessment, I want to congratulate you on all the work you have done to become happier, healthier, and more abundant. Because of the work you've done, you may have experienced significant shifts in one or more areas of your life; your health, your happiness, your relationship with yourself or others, your finances, or your work life. You may not be aware of all the changes that happened until you do some reflecting. One way to reflect on the past year and the progress you made is to go back and read through your responses to the exercises you did in this book.

I encourage you to use the information from the assessment and the reflection questions that follow as feedback. You can always go back and revisit any of the weekly readings to help support your future growth. At the back of the book is an index of the weekly readings in the following categories: Thoughts, Feelings, Giving and Receiving, Your Relationship with Yourself, and Fun, Play, and Enjoyment. The index will help you narrow down what weeks could be of benefit if you choose to work on one specific area.

Brain Makeover Follow-Up Assessment

Rate the following statements on a scale of 1-5.

A. My current level of overall satisfaction is (circle one)

1	2	3	4	5
none	low	moderate	elevated	high

B. My current level of overall happiness is (circle one)

1	2	3	4	5
none	low	moderate	elevated	high

C. My current level of overall stress is (circle one)

1	2	3	4	5
none	low	moderate	elevated	high

D. My current level of overall fear is (circle one)

1	2	3	4	5
none	low	moderate	elevated	high

E. When I think about my health, I feel (circle one)

1	2	3	4	5
fear	concern	neutral	good	happy

F. When I think about my finances, I feel (circle one)

1	2	3	4	5
fear	concern	neutral	good	happy

G. When I think about my relationships, I feel (circle one)

1	2	3	4	5
fear	concern	neutral	good	happy

The top three things I worry about are:

1. _____

2. _____

3. _____

Compare your results with the initial assessment you took at the beginning of the book.

Put a check mark next to each day that you take some time reflecting on what shifted for you over the course of the year by reviewing your responses in this book and answering the questions that follow.

_____ Day 1   _____ Day 4   _____ Day 7

_____ Day 2   _____ Day 5

_____ Day 3   _____ Day 6

Reflection Questions

1. What did you feel was the most powerful week for you? Why?

2. What did you learn about yourself?

3. What changed within you?

4. What did you learn about your relationships?

5. What did you learn about your patterns and your ability to shift them?

_____

_____

_____

_____

_____

_____

_____

_____

_____

Brain-Compatible New Year's Resolutions

From what you learned over the year, how are you going to take that forward? What commitment will you make to yourself next year? How will you reward yourself for the work that you did throughout the year with this book?

Think about what changes you want to make in the coming year. For your changes, or New Year's resolutions, to stick they must have significant meaning to you. Otherwise, they most likely will fall by the wayside quickly.

Here's an activity for you to do. On a piece of paper, make three columns for the following:

1. In column one, list one or two resolutions you are serious about.

2. In column two, write down some specifics about what's important to you about your resolutions.

3. In column three, write how you would feel if you carried out each resolution.

Next, imagine what it would look like and feel like to have what you desire. Picture it in your mind and feel it in your body. Then find, draw, or cut out a visual picture that captures your resolution and some feeling words to go with them.

To get your brain on board, you may want to create a "personal poster" with words and pictures that portray your resolution, and then focus on it for 18 seconds a day. Or, write down the feeling words and post them on your mirror or refrigerator to see multiple times a day.

Remember from It Only Takes 18 Seconds to Change Your Brain, Week 2 (on page 5), when you rehearse, imagine, or talk to yourself about something for 18 seconds, it gets stored in your long-term memory. This also keeps your thoughts congruent with your desires, and when this happens, it propels you toward activities and behaviors that produce the results you are looking for.

Gather your family or a friend or two and have fun creating meaningful resolutions for the New Year!

On Day 1 of this week, come up with one or two meaningful resolutions. Write how you would feel if you attained the results of your resolution. Then put a check mark next to each day that you imagine and feel (for 18 seconds) what it would be like to experience the end result of your resolution.

_____ Day 1   _____ Day 4   _____ Day 7

_____ Day 2   _____ Day 5

_____ Day 3   _____ Day 6

How was it to imagine and feel the end result of your resolution each day?

What's the first action step you will take to bring your meaningful resolution to fruition?

Can you come up with a realistic plan to make it happen? What would it look like?

Does it feel doable? If not, what thoughts and feelings are showing up? What are they telling you? What might you readjust so your brain is on board with your resolution?

_____

_____

_____

_____

_____

_____

_____

_____

_____

_____

_____

Acknowledgments

It brings me great pleasure to acknowledge the many people who helped me make this book possible. A big thanks go to my clients, family, friends, colleagues, and mentors. This second edition was a pleasure to write and edit with the support, encouragement, and input from Maura McCarly Torkelson!

Brain Makeover would not have come into form if it were not for Linda Loza, who got me started on the path of writing, by getting me set up with a blog. I remember sitting at her house on Easter Sunday as we created the site. Thank you for your generosity of time and talent to get me started!

A very special thank you goes to Lisa Rood, who lived this book with me. It was her inspiration and support along the way, and hours on the phone editing pages, that enriched this book.

Michael Ginsberg, my husband, quietly watched as I began writing. Somewhere along the way, he noticed my passion and often told me to make time to write. He knew how happy I was to make a difference in people's lives through my writing. Thank you for recognizing and supporting my dream!

My dad, Sam Mevorach, many times told me to think big, really big, and to take the metaphorical elevator with others who could help get me where I want to go with this book, rather than try to climb the steep mountain, by myself, and get dirty from falling down along the way. Thank you for being one of my biggest supporters!

My daughter, Stephanie Ginsberg, a Journalism Major in college, was able to put her editing skills into practice and offered some great suggestions. Thank you for your never-ending support!

Jennifer Kennedy, my daughter, who is a search engine marketing analyst, was extremely helpful in providing a beautifully detailed spreadsheet of tag words for the book. Thanks Jennifer! I can always count on you to make an impressive spreadsheet.

It was the eyes of Tambre Thompson who caught a couple of easy to overlook words that didn't belong. Thanks for meticulously reading through the manuscript and for your generous support!

It wouldn't have been possible to write *Brain Makeover* if I weren't willing to go through my own brain makeover and move beyond survival thinking.

Index of Brain Makeover Categories

Feelings

Fun, Play & Enjoyment

Giving & Receiving

Thoughts

Your Relationship with Yourself

PHYLLIS GINSBERG

Phyllis Ginsberg is known and beloved by lots of happier, less stressed working professionals as their Survival to Thrival Expert. She deploys her decades of training and experience as a marriage and family counselor with powerful lessons and tools gleaned from her lifelong passion for learning, to guide clients to make lasting, profound changes in their lives. Quickly, they shift their stressful thinking to achieve calm, clarity, and creativity. That means that the quality of their lives and work gets better – often in a moment's time. Phyllis and her husband live in the San Francisco Bay Area. For more information about Phyllis' work visit www.phyllisginsberg.com.

Contact Information

Website: phyllisginsberg.com

Email: phyllis@phyllisginsberg.com